# Effective Project Management

## by Patricia Brockett and Barbara Ettleson

American Media Publishing
4900 University Avenue
West Des Moines, IA 50266-6769 U.S.A.
800/262-2557
www.ammedia.com

# Effective Project Management

Patricia Brockett and Barbara Ettleson
Copyright © 1999 by American Media, Inc.

All rights reserved. No part of this publication may be reproduced, stored in a retrieval system, or transmitted, in any form or by any means, electronic, mechanical, photocopying, recording, or otherwise, without prior written permission of the publisher.

This publication is designed to provide accurate and authoritative information in regard to the subject matter covered. It is sold with the understanding that neither the author nor the publisher is engaged in rendering legal, accounting, or other professional service. If legal advice or other expert assistance is required, the services of a competent professional should be sought.

Credits:
American Media Publishing:         Art Bauer
                                   Todd McDonald
Editor in Chief:                   Karen Massetti Miller
Designer:                          Gayle O'Brien
Cover Design:                      Maura Rombalski

Published by American Media, Inc.
4900 University Avenue
West Des Moines, IA 50266-6769

Library of Congress Catalog Card Number 99-66179
Brockett, Patricia and Ettleson, Barbara
Effective Project Management

ISBN 1-884926-08-8

Printed in the United States of America
01 00 99           9 8 7 6 5 4 3 2 1

# Introduction

Though not a new concept, project management is becoming more widely used in all types of organizations. Today's ever-changing business environment requires organizations to add flexibility to their structure and methods of supervision.

Hierarchical organizations in which managers and supervisors maintain all control and assign all tasks are on the way out. Emerging in their place are customer-focused organizations that support and leverage the talents and skills of the workers who serve those customers.

The purpose of this book is to acquaint you with the basic skills and tools needed to manage a project. It will not substitute for experience, but it will help direct you to what works in various situations. We have adapted tried-and-true techniques and tools to today's fast-moving project management landscape where, instead of managing one project at a time, you may find yourself managing or involved in several at once.

Project management is on the rise, and qualified, capable project managers will be sought after in any organization. The materials covered in this book will give you a jump start toward joining the project manager ranks.

# About the Authors

Patricia Brockett has managed both Information Technology and other kinds of projects for governmental organizations in the State of Iowa for over 10 years. Her most recent work focuses on managing multiple projects within and across agency lines and frequently involves multiple partners from both the private and public sectors. Pat has taught project management and has employed these skills to assist nonprofit organizations with large fund-raising efforts.

Barbara Ettleson is President of Outcomes Unlimited, a management training and consulting firm in Des Moines, Iowa. Barb has provided training and consultation to clients throughout the U.S. in areas of organization development, interpersonal relationships, conflict management, strategic planning, team building, and many other subjects. Barb has managed in both project- and non-project-oriented environments and teaches project management skills to a variety of clients.

# Table of Contents

## Chapter One
### When Should You Use Project Management Techniques? — 6
- Project Management Versus Ongoing Management — 6
- Defining Your Project — 9
- Determining Your Project Framework — 12
- Assuming the Role of Project Manager — 13
- Chapter Summary — 16
- Self-Check: Chapter One Review — 18

## Chapter Two
### Tracking the Four Project Stages — 20
- Stage 1: Inception — 22
- Stage 2: Start-Up — 25
- Stage 3: Implementation — 27
- Stage 4: Close — 30
- Chapter Summary — 34
- Self-Check: Chapter Two Review — 35

## Stage 1: Inception — 37

## Chapter Three
### Determining the Project Structure — 38
- Working with the Appended Structure — 39
- Working with the Stand-Alone Structure — 43
- Working with the Partnership Structure — 47
- Chapter Summary — 52
- Self Check: Chapter Three Review — 53

## Chapter Four
### Measuring Project Success — 54
- Choosing Evaluation Criteria — 54
- Choosing a Structure: A Case Study — 58
- Chapter Summary — 60
- Self-Check: Chapter Four Review — 61

## Chapter Five
### Selecting the Project Manager — 62
- Managing the Appended Project — 64
- Managing the Stand-Alone Project — 64
- Managing the Partnership Project — 65
- What a Project Manager Needs to Know — 68
- Staffing the Project — 69
- Chapter Summary — 71
- Self-Check: Chapter Five Review — 72

## Stage 2: Start-Up — 75

### Chapter Six
## Planning the Project — 76
- Step 1: Identifying the Work Breakdown Structure — 77
- Step 2: Determining Task Relationships — 81
- Step 3: Creating the Network Diagram — 83
- Step 4: Establishing Time Needed — 89
- Step 5: Calculating the Expected Time — 90
- Step 6: Calculating the Time for Each Path — 92
- Step 7: Identifying the Critical Path — 92
- Step 8: Calculating the Slack — 94
- Step 9: Establishing the Timeline — 96
- Step 10: Setting the Project Budget — 98
- Chapter Summary — 99
- Self-Check: Chapter Six Review — 100

## Stage 3: Implementation — 103

### Chapter Seven
## Putting the Plan into Action — 104
- Monitoring Progress — 105
- Redesigning the Project Plan — 106
- Rescheduling Dates — 107
- Reallocating Resources — 108
- Delegating Tasks — 109
- Resolving Conflicts — 110
- Managing Interfaces — 113
- Chapter Summary — 114
- Self-Check: Chapter Seven Review — 115

## Stage 4: Close — 117

### Chapter Eight
## Concluding the Project — 118
- Resolving Project Commitments — 119
- Transferring Continuing Activities — 120
- Reassigning Project Personnel — 121
- Evaluating the Project — 123
- Pulling It All Together — 125
- Self-Check: Chapter Eight Review — 127

## Answers to Selected Exercises — 128

● When Should You Use Project Management Techniques?

# Chapter *One*

## When Should You Use Project Management Techniques?

> ### Chapter Objectives
> ▶ Distinguish between project and ongoing management.
> ▶ List the four factors that determine whether you are engaged in a project.
> ▶ Understand the framework in which the project manager operates.

Adding a new person to the team . . . Developing a new approach toward customer service . . . Organizing the annual picnic . . . Solving a complicated problem that involves people from across the organization . . . Providing employees with software training . . .

*Managing a project requires different skills and techniques than managing ongoing responsibilities.*

Which of these are projects and which of them are not? Managing a project requires different skills and techniques than managing ongoing responsibilities. The purpose of this chapter is to help you decide when a situation can be classified as a project and will therefore benefit from the project management techniques discussed in this book.

## Project Management Versus Ongoing Management

What is the difference between the responsibilities of managing an organizational unit and the responsibilities of managing a project? Let's consider the definitions of each:

*Ongoing management* implies a long-term investment aimed at meeting a constant need, whether that need be leasing space for the organization, processing incoming customer calls,

# When Should You Use Project Management Techniques?

reconciling statements of accounts, or any other function the organization routinely provides to its customers or staff. Usually a set of policies and procedures exists to guide the work of staff performing the function.

*Project management* implies a short-term investment aimed at meeting a time-sensitive, object-specific need that may never reoccur. That need could be reengineering the customer service function, creating and implementing the company's employee rewards system, or working with different units in the organization to determine how to improve the payroll process. Most often, no policies or procedures exist to guide the work of the project manager or project team.

Below are some examples of common factors shared by ongoing managers and project managers and an indication of how each of these factors is approached depending upon the type of management:

|  | Ongoing Management | Project Management |
| --- | --- | --- |
| Foundation | Rules/policies/procedures | Project plan |
| Time frame | Ongoing, long term | Project life, short term |
| Staffing | Permanent | Length of the project |
| Focus | Keeping things running smoothly | Making change |
| Authority base | Positional power | Personal influence |
| Risk factor | Low | High |

# When Should You Use Project Management Techniques?

All organizations have ongoing operational units. They require planning and thoughtful management to run smoothly and contribute to the organization's goals.

Day-to-day operational management is not project management; however, organizations will frequently try to have a manager do both. When projects are innocently inserted into the ongoing manager's life, both the project and the ongoing efforts may suffer.

Why is this true? One reason is that the skills and knowledge needed to run a smooth, efficient ongoing operation are not the same as those needed to run a fast-paced, high-risk, short-term project. Managers who enjoy and experience success in an ongoing management situation may not enjoy the project management environment.

Likewise, people who have spent much of their career managing projects frequently find themselves unsuccessful in managing an ongoing operation. Or they find that once the project becomes integrated into the ongoing structure of the organization, they become less involved and move on.

**Projects demand focused attention and constant status assessment.**

Another factor to consider is that projects demand focused attention and constant status assessment. When a manager tries to manage both a project and the ongoing needs of a unit, neither receives the attention it deserves, and neither the project team nor the organizational unit will be well managed.

But in the real world of organizations, chances are that managers, supervisors, and other professionals will be called upon to manage their ongoing workloads and projects at the same time. It becomes, therefore, even more important to know the difference between ongoing and project management responsibilities so that both the project and ongoing management work can effectively and successfully be completed.

# When Should You Use Project Management Techniques?

> **Take a Moment**
>
> 1. List four major duties or tasks that consume the majority of your work life right now.
>
>    a. _____
>
>    b. _____
>
>    c. _____
>
>    d. _____
>
> 2. Review the material you just read regarding ongoing management and project management. Now, returning to your list of four items, write below whether each falls under ongoing or project management and why.
>
>    a. _____
>
>    b. _____
>
>    c. _____
>
>    d. _____

## Defining Your Project

### What Do You Think?

- Sharon and Jim are discussing the assignments they received from their managers that morning. Sharon supervises a section responsible for the loading dock. They have expanded their dock size to load and unload three more trucks at a time and will be hiring new staff. The dock area has never had written procedures. Sharon's boss thinks that written procedures would make training these new employees easier and has asked Sharon to write them.

  Jim supervises an Information Technology unit. The company has decided to equip each of the 50 people in the accounting department with a personal computer. Jim's new assignment is to select the hardware and software, coordinate the purchase and installation, develop the training they'll need, and arrange for it to be delivered to each person receiving a personal computer.

# When Should You Use Project Management Techniques?

Which of these employees most needs to employ a project management approach to completing the assignment—Sharon or Jim?

Four factors can help you determine whether to initiate a project management approach or integrate tasks into an ongoing management system:

1. **Size**
   How big is the assignment? Is it a one-time undertaking, bigger than something your unit, department, or organization has ever done before? Are you buying one new piece of software or changing how one, two, or all of the systems will interact? Are you adding one person to a team or creating a whole new unit and set of services? The bigger the assignment, the more likely it is a project.

2. **Familiarity**
   Is the assignment unique or infrequent? If your unit always plans the annual picnic, doing next year's will probably not be a challenge. But if the boss asks your unit to organize the first charitable-giving drive for the entire organization, that is a challenge. Accomplishing this will require new planning, new tasks, and different time frames, and it will result in a different outcome. Due to its newness, this assignment is likely a project.

3. **Complexity**
   How many different points of coordination, collaboration, and interdependency are needed to accomplish this undertaking? If you have worked out the details of hiring new workers for your unit over the last few years, then hiring a new worker is a simple, routine process. But what about adding a whole new unit that has organization-wide responsibilities?

   Suddenly, the number of players involved increases, and the issues each player brings to the table make this a much more complex assignment. Projects often involve many people from many different internal organizational units. Projects may very well involve people from outside of the organization as well. The more complex the assignment, the more likely it is a project.

---

**Projects often involve many people from many different internal organizational units.**

# When Should You Use Project Management Techniques?

4. **Consequences**
   What happens if the implementation timelines for this assignment are delayed? What happens if the project is over budget? What happens if the customer is disappointed in your organization's performance? Is this a responsibility that will have a significant impact on how the unit, department, or organization operates? If the consequences would be considerable, the assignment is probably a project.

These four factors—size, familiarity, complexity, and consequences—define when an assignment should be considered a project. Interestingly, managers often begin new assignments without exploring these four factors. It is only when an assignment starts to go awry that they evaluate it and decide that approaching it as a project may help them salvage it. Sometimes this belated approach works—many times it doesn't. It is far more effective to decide early whether to use the methods of ongoing management or project management

> Size, familiarity, complexity, and consequences define when an assignment should be considered a project.

### Take a Moment

1. Review the four factors that can be used to determine if an assignment is a project or just part of your ongoing management responsibilities—size, familiarity, complexity, and consequences. Then reread the case study involving Sharon and Jim.

2. Based on your review and rereading, jot down at least three reasons why Jim should employ project management techniques and tools in completing his assignment.

   _____

   _____

   _____

# When Should You Use Project Management Techniques?

## Determining Your Project Framework

Once you have determined that an assignment will benefit from a project management approach, you need to determine the project's framework. A project's framework consists of three important characteristics:

- A defined goal that must be achieved within a certain period of time.

- Sequential and interrelated activities.

- A defined start and end point.

These characteristics are the components the project manager must define and effectively manage. Let's take a closer look at each:

- **Goal orientation**
  Each project has one overriding goal it is trying to accomplish. This becomes the sole focus for the project manager.

- **Coordinated undertaking of sequential and interrelated activities**
  Projects frequently involve many activities. These may be both sequential and simultaneous in nature. Organizing them into a coordinated project plan from which all team members can operate requires planning and flexibility.

- **Finite duration with beginning and end**
  One of the hallmarks of a project is that it has specific beginning and end points. It doesn't just fade away; there is a defined target date against which all activities get managed. This is a critical difference between projects and ongoing management tasks.

- **Urgency**
  Time is of the essence in a project. Projects are most often undertaken because of a pressing need. Meeting the project due date is often a major determinant of project success or failure.

> Each project has one overriding goal it is trying to accomplish.

# When Should You Use Project Management Techniques?

> **Take a Moment**
>
> 1. Recall a work or volunteer activity in which you have participated that was a coordinated effort, done in a short time frame, had definite start and end dates, and had a very specific and well-focused goal.
>
> 2. Below, write down as many activities as you can recall that met all four criteria.
>
> _____
>
> _____
>
> _____

## Assuming the Role of Project Manager

Project managers and ongoing managers each have a unique set of characteristics and talents. Frequently they are not the same characteristics and talents. Key characteristics of ongoing managers include:

- Enjoy routine.
- Feel comfortable with well-established policies and procedures.
- Prefer limited risk taking.
- Like a sense of permanence and a steady pace.
- Like long-term relationships.

*Project managers and ongoing managers each have a unique set of characteristics and talents.*

Project managers, on the other hand, display these key characteristics:

- Enjoy the challenge of doing something new.
- Like being a change agent.
- Like taking risks.
- Quickly develop new approaches and create detailed plans.
- Enjoy managing dynamic interfaces between people and systems.

## When Should You Use Project Management Techniques?

Thanks to their unique abilities, project managers are able to provide the focused attention needed for a complex, unfamiliar undertaking. If left within the normal organizational boundaries and assigned to an ongoing manager, this type of assignment will usually become buried among day-to-day business activities, go over budget, and not be completed by deadline, if at all. Project managers add value at a small price, and recognition of this role frequently makes the difference between success and failure of a project.

### The New Assignment: A Case Study

Leigh is the supervisor of a 15-person unit. She has held this position for three years and has helped the unit move from being a bottleneck that kept the organization from accomplishing its goals to an area other units turn to as a model of efficiency.

The organization is expanding, and Leigh's accomplishments have come to the attention of her management. She has just learned that she will organize a brand-new customer service unit. This will involve:
- Recommending the number and type of staff needed.
- Developing the job descriptions.
- Setting up where the unit will work.
- Organizing the training.
- Determining the processes and systems that will need to be developed.
- Determining how the unit will interact with the rest of the organization.

Leigh has only nine months before the unit is to be operational. She has talked with her manager, and they have decided that she will need assistance from Human Resources, Facilities Management, Information Technology, Communications, Training and Organizational Development, and the Quality Team.

# When Should You Use Project Management Techniques?

> **Take a Moment**
>
> 1. Is Leigh's assignment a project? Why or why not?
>
>    _____
>
>    _____
>
> 2. What will Leigh's manager gain by assigning this to Leigh as a project versus having her take it on as part of her ongoing management responsibilities?
>
>    _____
>
>    _____
>
> 3. Identify how the four factors that define a project (size, familiarity, complexity, consequences) are evidenced in a project you are working on or one that is being done in your organization.
>
>    _____
>
>    _____
>
> 4. Are you managing a project and performing ongoing management responsibilities at the same time? How is it working? Are there any changes you need to make?
>
>    _____
>
>    _____

# When Should You Use Project Management Techniques?

## Chapter Summary

Ongoing management implies a long-term investment aimed at meeting a constant need, whether that need be leasing space for the organization, processing incoming customer calls, reconciling statements of accounts, or any other function the organization routinely provides to its customers or staff. Usually a set of policies and procedures exists to guide the work of staff performing the function.

Project management implies a short-term investment aimed at meeting a time-sensitive, object-specific need that may never reoccur. That need could be reengineering the customer service function, creating and implementing the company's employee rewards system, or working with different units in the organization to determine how to improve the payroll processing. Most often, no policies or procedures exist to guide the work of the project manager or project team.

> **Ongoing management and project management are not the same.**

Ongoing management and project management are not the same. It is best for managers not to try to do both at the same time, as neither gets done well.

Four factors—size, familiarity, complexity, and consequences—determine whether an assignment should be considered a project. When an assignment is large, unfamiliar, complex, and has significant consequences, it could probably benefit from a project management approach.

Once you have determined that an assignment will benefit from a project management approach, you need to determine the project's framework. A project's framework consists of three important characteristics:

- A defined goal that must be achieved within a certain period of time.

- Sequential and interrelated activities.

- A defined start and end point.

These characteristics are the components the project manager must define and effectively manage.

## When Should You Use Project Management Techniques?

Project managers also have a unique set of characteristics that set them apart from ongoing managers. Effective project managers:

- Enjoy the challenge of doing something new.
- Like being a change agent.
- Like taking risks.
- Quickly develop new approaches and create detailed plans.
- Enjoy managing dynamic interfaces between people and systems.

Project managers add value at a small price, and recognition of this role frequently makes the difference between success and failure of a project.

## When Should You Use Project Management Techniques?

### Self Check: Chapter One Review

Answers to the following questions appear on page 128.

1. What is the difference between ongoing management and project management?

   _____

   _____

   _____

   _____

2. What four factors can help you determine whether an assignment is a project?

   a. _____

   b. _____

   c. _____

   d. _____

3. What are the three characteristics that determine a project's framework?

   a. _____

   b. _____

   c. _____

## When Should You Use Project Management Techniques?

4. Identify five skills that distinguish project managers from ongoing managers.

   a. _____

   b. _____

   c. _____

   d. _____

   e. _____

# Chapter Two
## Tracking the Four Project Stages

### Chapter Objectives
▶ Understand the four stages of each project.
▶ Know what tasks need to be accomplished in each stage.
▶ Graphically visualize a project.

For weeks, Chris has been hearing rumors about an important new project that her department, Research and Development, will be starting. Today, her manager has asked her to stop by and talk about it. Chris wonders if she is going to be asked to manage the project. If she were, where would she start? What would she need to know?

Chris's dilemma isn't that unusual. You may not know where to begin when you receive a new project management assignment. Fortunately, most projects break down into four identifiable stages:

1. Inception
2. Start-up
3. Implementation
4. Close

> **Most projects can be broken down into four easy-to-follow stages.**

Understanding the project stages will help you identify what tasks need to be accomplished and when they need to be completed.

Keep in mind, though, that you may not always begin work on a project in its Inception Stage. Project managers often find that they are assigned to a project later in the process—they find themselves starting not at the beginning of the project but in the middle. Inexperienced project managers may try to push ahead when they should take time to assess the situation, determine what tasks from previous stages still need to be completed, and decide how to proceed.

This chapter will help you identify the four project stages and what, at least ideally, needs to occur during each. The Project Stage Model on the following page helps by showing all the project stages and the tasks to be accomplished in each.

## Tracking the Four Project Stages

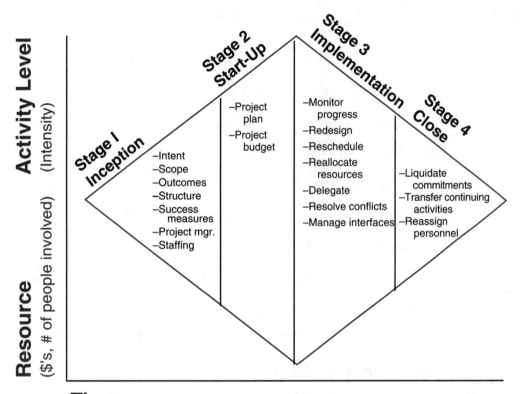

# Tracking the Four Project Stages

## Stage 1: Inception

**The Inception Stage includes tasks that are critical to the long-term viability of the project.**

Although not the longest of the four stages, the Inception Stage includes tasks that are critical to the long-term viability of the project. Decisions related to project structure, scope, and outcomes provide the foundation for the project—and the more solid that foundation, the greater the chance of project success. Ideally, the project manager is selected during the Inception Stage.

Tasks to be accomplished during this stage include:

1. Defining management's intent in undertaking the project.
2. Outlining the scope of the project.
3. Identifying desired outcomes.
4. Establishing the project organization.
5. Determining measures of success.
6. Selecting the project manager.
7. Selecting the project team members.

Let's return to the case study that was introduced at the beginning of this chapter to see the initial stage in action.

Case Study

### What Do You Think?

When Chris meets with her manager, Bob, he asks her to head up a project to reorganize the research and development lab. Bob explains that the company needs to cut its R & D time so new products are released into the market more quickly. The company is losing market share and needs to turn this trend around. Chris is excited because she has already identified several ways in which R & D processes could be improved and has discussed them with Bob.

Chris's project is to be a pilot that, if successful, will be duplicated in the company's other R & D units. She is being given nine months to cut R & D time for a single product from one year to six months. Because of the importance of the outcome and the short time frame in which to complete the project, she is being assigned to the project full time and will have a full-time team to assist her. At the end of nine months, she and her team are to have tested and prepared

## Tracking the Four Project Stages

recommendations for management on how R & D should be reorganized. Bob tells Chris he would like her to meet with the executive management team that afternoon to discuss what outcomes they expect from the project and to give her a chance to clarify any questions she might have. When they end their meeting, Chris is encouraged because management appears to support the project and will provide her with the resources to get the job done.

Chris's next task is to meet with Bob to select her team members. To do this, they will consider how the project will flow and what areas of the organization will be impacted. Those areas should be represented on the project team.

### Take a Moment

Describe how the Stage 1 tasks have been addressed in Chris's project:

Defining management's intent

_____

_____

Outlining the scope of the project

_____

_____

Identifying desired outcomes

_____

_____

*continued on next page*

## Tracking the Four Project Stages

**Take a Moment** *(continued)*

Establishing the project organization

_____
_____
_____

Determining measures of success

_____
_____
_____

Selecting the project manager

_____
_____
_____

Selecting team members

_____
_____
_____

Let's check your understanding of the tasks:

- **Management's intent**
  Management wants to cut research and development time so new products are released into the market more quickly.

- **Project scope**
  The project is to last nine months and is to deal primarily with the R & D area of the company.

- **Desired outcome**
  Management wants to reduce the time it takes to develop a product from one year to six months.

- **Project organization**
  The project is to be organized with a full-time project manager and a full-time team reporting directly to the project manager.

# Tracking the Four Project Stages

- **Measures of success**
  Chris and her team are responsible for testing their recommendations and reporting them to management at the end of the nine-month period.

- **Selection of project manager**
  The fact that Chris has already been suggesting ways to improve the lab was probably one reason she was selected to be the project manager.

- **Selection of team members**
  To determine the team's makeup, Chris and Bob identify what areas of the organization will be impacted by the project and choose team members who can represent these areas and accomplish the types of tasks that will be required.

## Stage 2: Start-Up

The Start-Up Stage should take about as long as the Inception Stage. This stage builds on the Stage 1 foundation by:

1. Creating the project plan

2. Setting the project budget

Let's return to our case study to see how these tasks are accomplished.

> The Start-Up Stage should take about as long as the Inception Stage.

### What Do You Think?

Chris and Bob have selected her project team. They decided that Chris's team should include a member from marketing, a member from information technology, and several members from Chris's own area of research and design. Chris will meet with her team to determine what tasks need to be done, who will do them, and how they will be accomplished. After Chris and her team identify the tasks necessary to complete the project, they may decide to add more team members from other areas. Chris has also asked that someone from the finance area attend these planning sessions to help the team prepare the budget.

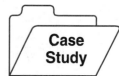
Case Study

## ● Tracking the Four Project Stages

### Take a Moment

Describe how the Stage 2 tasks have been addressed in Chris's project:

Creating a project plan

_____

_____

Setting the project budget

_____

_____

Think about a project with which you have been involved. Describe the process that was used in developing the project plan. Do you think the project team consisted of the right members? What level of detail was used to identify the costs for the budget?

_____

_____

_____

_____

Let's check your understanding of the tasks:

- **Creating the project plan**
  Chris's team will help her determine what specific tasks need to be done and who should do them. To do this, they will need to consider how the tasks relate to each other and how much time each task will take.

- **Setting the budget**
  Chris and her team will develop the budget together. Although not an official member of the team, a representative of the finance department will help with the creation of the project budget.

# Tracking the Four Project Stages

## Stage 3: Implementation

The Implementation Stage is the longest stage of the project—and if you don't adequately complete Stages 1 or 2, Stage 3 can seem endless. In the Implementation Stage, your ability to manage multiple tasks, people issues, and organizational interfaces will be challenged. Fast turnaround and consistent monitoring are critical to project success.

> **If you don't adequately complete Stages 1 or 2, Stage 3 can seem endless.**

Tasks to be accomplished during this stage include:

1. Monitoring progress
2. Redesigning the project plan
3. Rescheduling dates
4. Reallocating resources
5. Delegating tasks
6. Resolving conflicts
7. Managing interfaces

Let's see how Chris accomplishes these tasks in her project.

## What Do You Think?

It's Friday, and Chris is checking her calendar, reviewing all of the things she has to do today.

On Fridays, she meets with her team for their weekly status report. This meeting brings everyone up to date on the team's progress, any problems that have occurred and their impact on the project schedule, and any changes that need to be made to the project plan in order to stay on schedule.

Case Study

Thanks to these meetings, Chris was able to identify a complication that would have affected her project's completion date. Because she caught the problem early, she was able to hire some temporary staff members to help the work stay on schedule.

After the project team's status meeting, Chris will meet with two of the team members to help them resolve a conflict that they are having. Hector has been complaining that Zakia is not getting her tasks done, and this is causing him to fall behind on his. The

## Tracking the Four Project Stages

project team may have underestimated the amount of work involved in Zakia's tasks.

Jane, on the other hand, is ahead of schedule on her tasks, so she could be reassigned to assist Zakia. Zakia may also be having problems getting the information she needs from the production department. Since Roger came from production, Chris bets he could grease some wheels if given the assignment.

Then there is the meeting scheduled with the finance department to go over the project's budget and expenses to date. Chris may have to do some creative thinking at this meeting because the unexpected need for temporary help threw the budget off.

This is the last day of the month, when Chris reports to the company's vice presidents on the status of the project. Last week she met with the department heads that report to the VPs, so there should not be any surprises when Chris finishes with today's update that everything is on schedule.

### Take a Moment

Review Chris's planning for the day and record where and how each of the tasks in Stage 3 is included.

Monitoring progress

_____

_____

Redesigning the project plan

_____

_____

*continued on next page*

# Tracking the Four Project Stages

**Take a Moment** *(continued)*

Rescheduling dates

___

Reallocating resources

___

Delegating tasks

___

Resolving conflicts

___

Managing interfaces

___

Chris seems to have her project under control and has done all of the tasks in this stage at least once.

- **Monitoring progress**
  Chris monitors the project's progress at a weekly status meeting.

- **Redesigning the project plan and reallocating resources**
  As a result of her weekly status meetings, Chris redesigned the project plan when she called in temporary staff members for assistance. This resulted in an unforeseen expenditure

that will now cause a reallocation of resources to keep the project within budget.

- **Rescheduling commitments, delegating tasks, and resolving conflicts**
  Chris will reschedule team members' time by asking Jane to assist Zakia and delegating the contact with production to Roger. This will also help resolve the conflict between Hector and Zakia.

- **Managing interfaces**
  Finally, there are several interfaces that Chris must manage: other departments (production and finance), department heads, and the VPs.

Did you identify all of these tasks in your review of the case study?

## Stage 4: Close

Project managers frequently don't think about the close of their project until it occurs. But if you follow the project management approach described in the following chapters, you will actually have your close planned once you determine the project's structure, scope, and measures of success in Stage 1.

> **The close determines how the results of a project continue to live and grow.**

Although briefer than any of the other stages, the close is still important because it determines how the results of a project continue to live and grow either within the organization or as a spin-off from the organization. Or, if the project was canceled, how the lessons learned are captured for future use. This stage is also about the people who have worked on the project and how their futures are secured or assisted.

Tasks to be accomplished during this stage include:

1. Resolving project commitments.

2. Transferring continuing activities.

3. Reassigning project personnel.

4. Conducting a project evaluation.

## Tracking the Four Project Stages

Let's see how Chris and her team close their project.

## What Do You Think?

Chris and her team had worked together for the past several months redesigning and implementing the new research and development processes for the company. Beginning Monday, they would all move on to their next assignments. But tonight, the company vice presidents were hosting the team to a congratulatory dinner and public recognition of their successful accomplishments.

The project team had been located off site from the company headquarters, and this isolation had added to their development as a high functioning team and their ability to concentrate exclusively on the project. During the last week, Chris had spent a lot of her time following up with their landlord to ensure that the lease would be terminated at the end of the month. She had cancelled the telephones, arranged to have the copy machines, files, and furniture moved back to headquarters, and asked the information technology staff to remove their personal computers.

The rest of the team spent the last week finishing up with the last portion of the project plan—training for production personnel in the new processes. Everything had gone smoothly, and it was gratifying to see the fruits of their labor becoming a reality.

None of the team members was anxious regarding what he or she would be doing on Monday. When the project team was formed, each team member had been given the assignment that would be waiting for him or her at the end of the project. As the project continued and the needs of the organization shifted, any changes in these assignments had been planned and communicated. Chris had seen this as part of her job as the project manager, and it was allowing for a very smooth transition.

## Tracking the Four Project Stages

### Take a Moment

How are Chris and her team completing the tasks associated with the close of a project?

Resolving project commitments

_____
_____

Transferring continuing activities

_____
_____

Reassigning project personnel

_____
_____

Have you been involved in a project that did not end as smoothly as Chris's? Take a minute and jot down why you think your project ended as it did.

_____
_____
_____
_____

## Tracking the Four Project Stages

Let's check your understanding of the tasks:

- **Resolving project commitments**
  Because Chris and her team were housed away from the company headquarters, she had to discontinue and cancel some resources. These included the building lease and the telephones. She also arranged to have the copy machines, furniture, and PCs returned to headquarters.

- **Transferring continuing activities**
  Chris's project was a particular success because its close had not been left as an afterthought. The project team was conducting final training as Chris dealt with the tasks to close the project down.

- **Reassigning project personnel**
  Because of the foresight that Chris and the company managers had as to what would happen at the end of the project, all of the team members knew where they would report once the project ended. This added to the success of the project because Chris and the team members could devote all of their attention to the project up to the very end, rather than worrying about looking for other work and possibly leaving the team for other opportunities before its completion.

In this chapter, we've considered each of the four stages of a project. These stages and the tasks they involve remain consistent across most types of projects. In the chapters that follow, we'll take a look at how the various stages operate in a variety of project structures.

● **Tracking the Four Project Stages**

## Chapter Summary

Organizing your project by stages will help you identify what tasks need to be accomplished and when they need to be completed. Most projects can be broken down into four stages:

1. Inception
    - Defining management's intent in undertaking the project.
    - Outlining the scope of the project.
    - Identifying desired outcomes.
    - Establishing the project organization
    - Determining measures of success.
    - Selecting the project manager.

2. Start-up
    - Determining how to staff the project.
    - Creating the project plan.
    - Creating the project budget.

3. Implementation
    - Monitoring progress.
    - Redesigning the project plan.
    - Rescheduling dates.
    - Reallocating resources.
    - Delegating tasks.
    - Resolving conflicts.
    - Managing interfaces.

4. Close
    - Resolving project commitments.
    - Transferring continuing activities.
    - Reassigning project personnel.
    - Conducting a project evaluation.

# Tracking the Four Project Stages

## Self Check: Chapter Two Review

Answers to the following questions appear on page 128-129.

Match the following project management stages with the tasks below.

A. Stage 1: Inception
B. Stage 2: Start-up
C. Stage 3: Implementation
D. Stage 4: Close

\_\_\_ 1. Defining management's intent in undertaking the project

\_\_\_ 2. Creating the project plan

\_\_\_ 3. Resolving project commitments

\_\_\_ 4. Reallocating resources

\_\_\_ 5. Monitoring progress

\_\_\_ 6. Identifying the desired outcomes

\_\_\_ 7. Creating the project budget

\_\_\_ 8. Outlining the scope of the project

\_\_\_ 9. Transferring continuing activities

\_\_\_ 10. Resolving conflicts

\_\_\_ 11. Establishing the project organization

\_\_\_ 12. Selecting the project manager

\_\_\_ 13. Selecting the project staff

\_\_\_ 14. Redesigning the project plan

\_\_\_ 15. Delegating tasks

\_\_\_ 16. Reassigning project personnel

\_\_\_ 17. Managing interfaces

\_\_\_ 18. Determining measures of success

\_\_\_ 19. Rescheduling dates

# Stage 1: Inception

Though Stage 1 is not the longest stage in the project development process, it is probably the most critical to project success. Unless the tasks in the Inception Stage are successfully completed, the following stages will lack direction and focus. Therefore, we will devote the next five chapters to considering the following Stage 1 tasks:

- Determining the project structure

- Establishing measurements for project success

- Selecting a project manager

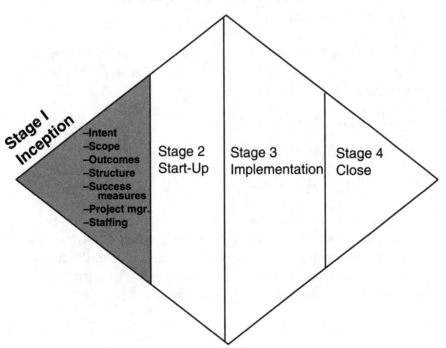

# Chapter Three
## *Determining the Project Structure*

### Chapter Objectives

▶ Recognize the Appended, Stand-Alone, and Partnership Project Structures.

▶ Describe each structure's benefits and challenges.

▶ Recognize situations in which each structure is most effective.

In our previous chapter, we considered the four project stages and the tasks that need to be completed in each. Familiarity with these stages and tasks will help you bring your project to a successful completion, no matter when you enter the project management process.

An important task that takes place in the Inception Stage is determining what structure your project will have. There are three basic ways of structuring a project:

- The Appended Project Structure
- The Stand-Alone Structure
- The Partnership Structure

*Each type of structure offers a number of benefits and also presents a number of challenges.*

Each type of structure offers a number of benefits and also presents a number of challenges. Even if you are not responsible for deciding which structure your project will use, if you are able to identify your project's structure, you can capitalize on that structure's benefits and prepare for its challenges.

# Determining the Project Structure

## Working with the Appended Structure

As we saw previously, a project has the best chance for success when it is assigned to a project manager who is not responsible for ongoing managerial duties. Unfortunately, this type of assignment is not always possible. When the project manager and project team members are given responsibility for a project without being relieved of any day-to-day responsibilities, the project has an Appended Structure. The project assignment is added, or appended, to an already full workload.

**In an Appended Structure, the project is added to a full workload.**

Let's see how the Appended Structure works in this case study:

## The First Special Project: A Case Study

Cindy is the manager of the accounts receivable area in a medium-size printing company. The employees are treated very well, but they are not given much latitude for independent, creative thinking. Many of the company's operations have been done in the same manner for the past 20 years. However, management realizes that the company must change to compete in the changing marketplace.

Cindy has been directed by her vice president to evaluate and redo the process used to monitor and follow up on overdue accounts. Because specialized efforts like this are new to the company, there is little money in the budget to accomplish this project. Even so, the project's success is important to the company. Top management thinks that developing more efficiency in this area could save the company an amount equal to 10 percent of their operating budget per year in lost investment opportunities.

The vice president has selected five staff people who directly report to Cindy to be the project team. Cindy will act as the project manager even though she has never managed a project like this before. Because of the close supervision that she has always received from her vice president, the project's major financial impact to the company, and the company's lack of experience with projects, Cindy's vice president will take an active interest in the management of the project.

39

• **Determining the Project Structure**

### "Appended" Means Adding Responsibilities

The project that Cindy has been given is organized in an Appended Structure because Cindy and her staff are not relieved of any of their current duties and responsibilities.

**A project with an Appended Structure is often placed in a particular functional area.**

A project with an Appended Structure is often placed in a particular functional area, like the accounts receivable area in our case study (see diagram 3.1). The project manager is often a manager or staff member in that area selected because of technical expertise. In our example, Cindy was selected because she has managed the accounts receivable area, and this is the area targeted for change as a result of the project.

**Diagram 3.1:**

# Appended Project Structure

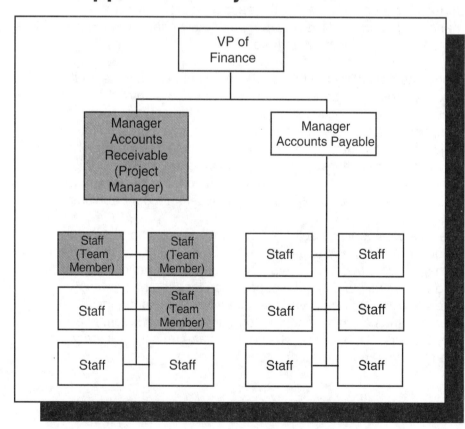

## Determining the Project Structure

Like Cindy, the person selected as the project manager may know little about managing a project. The project assignment may come as a delegation or abdication from a higher-level manager who doesn't have time to deal with this project because of the demands of his or her own workload. This manager continues to maintain control over how the project is progressing. This manager is the sponsor of the project.

### Benefits and Challenges of the Appended Structure

Like all of the project structures, the Appended Structure offers both benefits and challenges to the organization and the project manager, as the following table illustrates.

| Benefits | Challenges |
| --- | --- |
| Clearly defined authority among project sponsor, project manager, and team members leads to better control. | If team members come from only one functional area, they may have a narrow perspective on the project. |
| Project manager can call on authority of project sponsor to get tasks done. | The interests of the team members' functional area may take precedence over broader organizational goals. |
| Close physical proximity of team members improves communication. | Interdepartmental rivalry and limited cooperation with other organizational units may develop. |
| High technical competence of team reduces learning curve. | Because project tasks are added to existing responsibilities, the project may get limited attention from the project team. |

# Determining the Project Structure

## When to Use the Appended Structure

- When the organization believes it cannot afford (either financially or interpersonally) to disrupt its existing organization structure.

- When the organization rarely has projects and is not aware of other options for organizing these specialized efforts.

- When a project is regarded as "nice" but not critical to the organization's future.

- When organizational control and functional accountability (each manager of an area taking responsibility for everything that happens in that area) are important to the organization.

**Take a Moment**

Review the opening case study about Cindy's project at the printing company and answer the following questions.

1. List three reasons why the Appended Structure may be appropriate for the printing company.

   _____

   _____

   _____

2. List two potential problems that the Appended Structure may cause during the course of Cindy's project.

   _____

   _____

# Determining the Project Structure

Did you identify these points as the reasons why the appended structure may be appropriate for this company?

- This is one of the first projects that the company has undertaken, so it has limited knowledge of project organization options.

- The fact that Cindy's vice president will be so involved in the management of the project exemplifies the company's "control" philosophy and culture.

- Management of the project is simplified by keeping the project team in the same physical proximity and normal chain of command. This may be helpful since the company has few resources to expend on the project, and it is inexperienced in project management.

Did you identify any others?

Here are two of the potential problems that might occur as a result of using this structure. Can you think of others?

- The project may not be completed by its due date because the team may have difficulty accomplishing project tasks on top of their daily responsibilities.

- Because other areas of the company that may be impacted by procedural changes in the accounts receivable area are not represented on the team, there could be interdepartmental rivalry and limited cooperation, undermining the successful completion of the project.

## Working with the Stand-Alone Structure

Kumari has been asked to develop and implement a new approach to customer service in the credit card division of a large bank. The project involves not only developing a new approach to customer service, but also a new product that, if successful, will revolutionize the credit card industry.

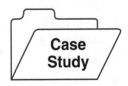
Case Study

The credit card division has lost a large portion of its market share to its competitors over the last year, and this project is seen as the way to save the business. Because of its critical importance to the future of the organization, the project has been given top priority

# Determining the Project Structure

within the company. It has been set up as a separate department with Kumari reporting to the company CEO and serving on the executive management team with the other department heads.

In order to attract the best and brightest from within and outside of the organization to this team, the project has been given a lot of flexibility as to salary, job classification, and duties. If Kumari needs a type of skill or knowledge not found within the company's current staff, she can create a special position and hire the staff she needs from the outside.

Although the project is located in the same building as the rest of the credit card division, it has been physically set apart in its own wing on one floor of the building.

The bank has invested a tremendous amount of money in Kumari's project. It has hired an internationally recognized consulting firm for advice on the type of new product to develop and how this can be done within the company's current organizational structure.

The positions the internal team members left when assigned to the project team have been filled so that the operation of the other lines of division business have not suffered during the project duration. This also means that when the project ends, or if the project fails, there is no guarantee that the team members will be able to move back to their old jobs. However, because of the frequent employee turnover in the credit card business, management feels confident that there will be jobs available for all team members if the project is disbanded.

> In a Stand-Alone Structure, team members are removed from their areas of functional responsibility to devote 100 percent of their time to the project.

## "Stand-Alone" Means Independent

Kumari's project is an example of the Stand-Alone Structure. Such a project may stand alone within the larger organization with some links to shared resources that sponsors don't want to duplicate (i.e. information technology, accounting, etc.). Or the project may be totally on its own with the resources to acquire all that it needs. The project team members are removed from their areas of functional responsibility to devote 100 percent of their time to the project. A Stand-Alone Structure would look like Diagram 3.2 on the following page.

# Determining the Project Structure

## Diagram 3.2:
## Stand-Alone Project Structure

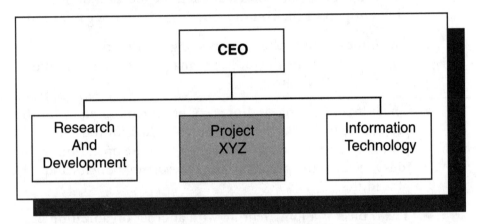

### Benefits and Challenges of the Stand-Alone Structure

| Benefits | Challenges |
|---|---|
| Other organizational units consider the project a top priority. | Resentment and jealousy may develop over the Stand-Alone project's special treatment. |
| The project manager's authority and responsibility is maximized. | Administrative matters may take up a lot of the project manager's time and distract him or her from project issues. |
| Project team members focus solely on the project, allowing them to quickly adapt to changing needs. | It may be difficult to recruit team members because employees may be concerned about employment options after the project terminates. |
| Project team members and others who work with the project can easily understand its structure. | Because it requires a separate staff, the Stand-Alone structure is the most costly structure. |
| New policies and practices are developed to meet the project's special needs. | Developing new policies and procedures takes away time from management project outcomes. |

# Determining the Project Structure

## When to Use the Stand-Alone Structure

Use the Stand-Alone Structure when:

- The project is being housed at a remote location or in a different part of the country from the existing organization.

- The importance of the project is so great that the organization wants the project manager to have maximum control and flexibility.

- The human resource and/or accounting requirements for the project are significantly different from those of the parent company, and it is easier to set up a separate operation than to try to force the project to use the existing policies and procedures.

- The project is a joint venture with another organization or company. By organizing the project as a stand-alone, the focus of the effort will be maximized for both participants.

### Take a Moment

Review the project scenario involving Kumari at the beginning of this section. Based on this and the information describing the Stand-Alone Structure, answer the following questions:

1. What makes the structure of the credit card division's project Stand-Alone?

   _____

   _____

2. Why do you think this project structure was selected over the Appended Structure?

   _____

   _____

What were the reasons that you identified that make this a Stand-Alone project? Did they include the following?

- The project team members report directly to the project manager and spend 100 percent of their time on the project.

# Determining the Project Structure

- Special organizational procedures have been developed that allow Kumari more flexibility in hiring and salaries paid to meet the unique requirements of the project.

- The project visibility is high as illustrated by Kumari being given the status of a department head and member of the executive management team.

Did the reasons you identified as to why the Stand-Alone project structure was selected include any of the following?

- The importance to the future of the company of the development of this new product justifies the large financial commitment that the company has made.

- The presence of the international consulting firm has created a "partnership" with the company, and the company wants to get as much value from the consultants' time as possible. The dedication of their own full-time staff is the best way to accomplish this.

- The need by the company for this project to be completed by the projected deadline is critical enough that the company willingly dedicates full-time staff to accomplish it.

## Working with the Partnership Structure

**Case Study**

Dave took over the management of a project two months ago. The project had been going on for a year but had been floundering, and there was concern that it would not be completed on time. So Dave's boss asked him to step in as project manager, evaluate the status, and report back to the executive management team with his recommendations.

The project that Dave inherited was organized in the partnership structure. This project team was composed of 10 employees whose regular work assignments were in the departments of finance, accounting, sales, manufacturing, research and development, information technology, and customer service. This meant seven different supervisors and departments also had a minimum of 50 percent of the team members' time.

Not all of the departmental managers viewed the project with the same sense of urgency as the executive team. Over the course of the project, team members had complained that their operational supervisors would not always ease up on their assignments to allow them to complete project tasks.

# Determining the Project Structure

With only nine months before the project completion date, Dave began his evaluation by looking at the original scope and outcomes to determine how realistic they now were considering the approaching completion date and the remaining project budget. What he discovered was not encouraging.

The outcome that could be achieved within the remaining time and budget was about 30 percent of what had been promised. The achievements that would be most exciting to customers would need an additional 18 months to be accomplished under the current partnership project structure.

In Dave's view, the primary problem was with the project structure. The project outcomes were attainable considering the talent within the company. It was how the company was willing to achieve those outcomes and the resources it was willing to invest in the project that were now the issue.

## "Partnership" Means Working Together

Within the Partnership Structure, the project team members spend a portion of their time working on the project and a portion of their time on their regular responsibilities. They report to both their regular supervisor and the project manager. In our previous case study, Dave had only 50 percent of his team members' time. The rest of their time they continued with their regular job duties.

In a Partnership project, the project manager and team members may be drawn from anywhere in the organization. The project manager is usually relieved of other ongoing responsibilities in order to focus on the project. Though the project manager takes responsibility for completing the project, she or he does not take on personnel responsibilities for the team members, such as performance appraisals, replacing staff if they quit, etc.

Personnel responsibilities remain with the regular supervisors to whom team members still report. In organizations with clear corporate goals where teams are common and territorial boundaries are low, the Partnership Structure works extremely well. As you can see by Diagram 3.3, in a Partnership Structure, team members are accountable to two people: their regular supervisors for their ongoing responsibilities and the project manager for their project-specific duties. The team members split their time between the project and their ongoing responsibilities.

> Within the Partnership Structure, the project team members spend a portion of their time working on the project and a portion of their time on their regular responsibilities.

# Determining the Project Structure

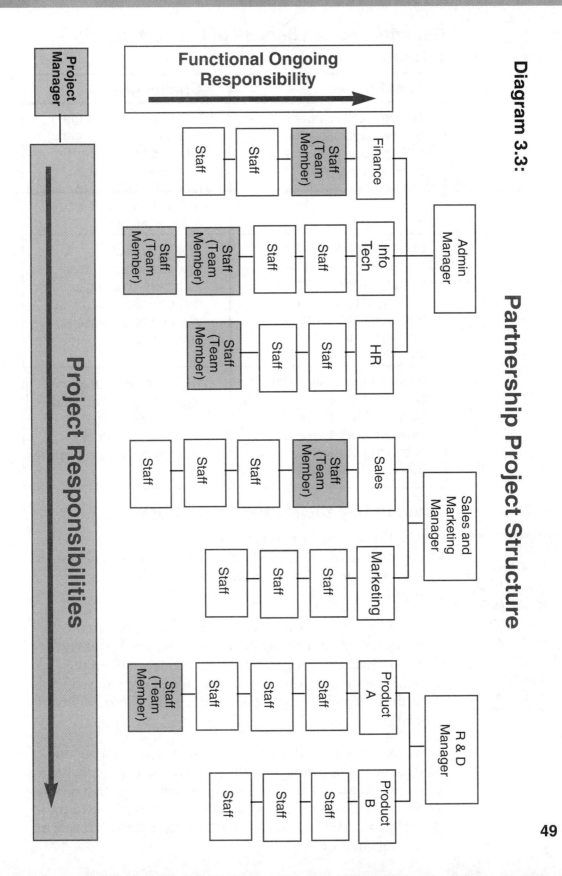

Diagram 3.3: Partnership Project Structure

# Determining the Project Structure

## Benefits and Challenges of the Partnership Structure

| Benefits | Challenges |
| --- | --- |
| The project manager is clearly responsible for project leadership and monitors progress. | Though the role of the project manager is clear, other aspects of the Partnership Structure may be confusing to people both inside and outside the team. |
| Because team members retain their ongoing jobs, the structure maximizes the use of personnel resources and gives employees a sense of stability. | Adding project responsibilities to team members' ongoing job responsibilities can result in poor performance in both areas. |
| Because team members come from different functional areas, the structure opens up lines of communication between those areas. | Team members' dual responsibilities can lead to conflicts around authority, resources, recognition, and rewards. |

## When to Use the Partnership Structure

> **Use the Partnership Structure when a project cuts across many issues and functions within the organization.**

Use the Partnership Structure when:

- A project demands a dual- or multiple-level focus because it cuts across many issues and functions within the organization.

- Resources are not available to be dedicated solely to the project; they must be shared among functional areas and the project. Using a Partnership Structure will keep the organization operating effectively, though at a reduced level in the functional areas because of the reduced availability of staff time.

- Many kinds of sophisticated skills are needed in designing, testing, and implementing the project, and these skills are located in various parts of the organization. The Partnership Structure allows for the needed skills to be available to the project and not be completely lost to the operational side of the organization.

## Determining the Project Structure

> ### Take a Moment
> 1. Based on your understanding of the Partnership Structure, its benefits and challenges, and the reasons why one would select this over the others, what structure would you now recommend be used in Dave's project (described at the beginning of the chapter) and why?
>
> _____
>
> _____
>
> 2. What was the reason presented in the case study as to why the partnership structure did not work?
>
> _____
>
> _____

Did you identify Stand-Alone as the new structure that would best enable Dave's project to reach its goals? The primary reasons are that the timetable has become so tight that the project tasks must have the full-time attention of the project team in order to be completed on time.

Of course the company may not be willing to dedicate the amount of personnel time that is required for a Stand-Alone Structure. The company may instead decide to abandon the project (which would leave many unhappy customers), or it may reduce the expected outcomes so something can be accomplished within the present structure, budget, and deadline.

Another alternative might be to assign team members full-time to the project until it is caught up without permanently changing the project structure.

We have seen three different ways to structure a project. Understanding the way your project is structured can help you identify benefits that will help you complete the project as well as challenges that could hinder your progress. Once you have determined how your project is structured, you can use what you know about that structure to help you determine how you will measure your project's success. We'll talk more about measuring success in the next chapter.

# Determining the Project Structure

## Chapter Summary

Recognizing your project's structure will help you identify the benefits it offers and the challenges it presents. There are three basic project structures:

- The Appended Structure
- The Stand-Alone Structure
- The Partnership Structure

Organizations often use an Appended Structure when:

- The project does not require new staff or other additional resources.
- The organization is unfamiliar with project management and is unaware of other options.
- The project is not critical to the functioning of the company.
- The organization's management values control and functional accountability.

Organizations often use a Stand-Alone Structure when:

- The project is not housed with the rest of the company.
- The project's results are critical to the company.
- The project team would have difficulty functioning if it were required to follow current company policies and procedures.
- The project is a joint venture with another organization outside of the company.

Organizations often use a Partnership Structure when:

- A project demands a dual or multilevel focus that cuts across many issues and functions within an organization.
- Resources are not available to be dedicated solely to the project.
- Many different skills are needed to successfully complete the project, and these skills are scattered throughout the organization.

# Determining the Project Structure

## Self-Check: Chapter Three Review

Answers appear on page 129.

When should you use the three basic project structures? Match the various situations with the correct structure.

A. The Appended Structure
B. The Stand-Alone Structure
C. The Partnership Structure

___ 1. The project is not housed with the rest of the company.

___ 2. The project is not critical to the functioning of the company.

___ 3. The project demands a multilevel focus that cuts across many issues and functions within the organization.

___ 4. The organization's management values control and functional accountability.

___ 5. The project team would have difficulty functioning if it were required to follow current company policies and procedures.

___ 6. The project is a joint venture with another organization outside of the company.

___ 7. Many different skills are needed to successfully complete the project, and these skills are scattered throughout the organization.

___ 8. The organization is unfamiliar with project management.

___ 9. The project's results are critical to the company.

• **Measuring Project Success**

# Chapter *Four*

## *Measuring Project Success*

### Chapter Objectives

▶ Identify the measures of project success.

▶ Explain the impact of the project structure on project success measures.

**Case Study**

Grand Oaks, a large metropolitan city in the Midwest, is struggling to survive. Residents are moving to the suburbs to escape crime, high taxes, and declining public schools. To combat this urban flight, city residents have formed neighborhood associations to bring their concerns to city government. The city council sees the neighborhood associations as positive forces within the city and is looking for ways to work with them.

One program that the city hopes will involve the neighborhood associations is the establishment of neighborhood gardens. The city has hired Sarah Bennett to develop the neighborhood garden program. The gardens will serve multiple purposes:
- Make unused city land available to local residents.
- Beautify and improve neighborhood eyesores.
- Provide opportunities for neighborhoods to develop and enhance their identity by encouraging neighbors to work together.

Sarah has been given the resources to hire staff to help her coordinate this project, but will also need volunteer support from the city's various neighborhoods. As she begins work, she wonders, "How can I measure whether the project is a success, and how will the city decide whether I've succeeded?"

## Choosing Evaluation Criteria

During the Inception Stage, the organization and the project manager should determine how they will measure the success of the project when it is done. There are two different sets of criteria that may be used to determine whether a project has been successful:

# Measuring Project Success

- Whether project tasks are accomplished
- How the project is managed

The type of project structure selected greatly influences whether a project can successfully meet either set of criteria. Let's look at each set of success criteria and consider how various project structures support it.

## Accomplishing Project Tasks

What are the most important tasks the project needs to accomplish? Will the project structure support those tasks? The following table lists some common tasks that can influence a project's success and the project structures that best support them:

> The type of project structure selected greatly influences whether a project can successfully meet either set of criteria.

| Criteria for Success | Structure That Best Supports | Next Most Effective Structure | Least Effective Structure |
|---|---|---|---|
| **Meeting Deadlines:** Will there be serious consequences if the project misses its deadline? | Stand-Alone | Partnership | Appended |
| **Implementing Outcomes:** Does the organization's future depend on successfully implementing project outcomes? | Partnership | Stand-Alone | Appended |
| **Maintaining Customer Confidence:** Is internal and external customer confidence in project results crucial to the organization? | Stand-Alone | Partnership | Appended |
| **Creating Change:** Is it critical that change created by the project be institutionalized within the organization? | Stand-Alone | Partnership | Appended |

# Measuring Project Success

## Managing the Project

Many organizations are concerned with how a project was managed and whether positive relationships inside and outside the organization were maintained. Once again, the project structure influences how effectively these criteria can be met:

| Criteria for Success | Structure That Best Supports | Next Most Effective Structure | Least Effective Structure |
|---|---|---|---|
| **Gaining Buy-In:** Did the project team develop relationships with key areas inside and outside the organization to create support for the project? | Partnership | Stand-Alone | Appended |
| **Providing Access:** Was information about project progress made available to others within the organization? Were project team members given access to needed resources? | Stand-Alone | Partnership | Appended |
| **Managing Risk:** Do project team members feel secure about their jobs? | Appended | Partnership | Stand-Alone |
| **Providing Closure:** Will the project spin off on its own to become a new organizational unit? Will the changes begun by the project move into an existing unit? Or will the project simply end? | Stand-Alone (Most effective if project is to spin off on its own.) | Partnership (Most effective if changes will move into an existing unit.) | Appended (Most effective if project will simply end.) |

As you can see, you could have a very difficult time meeting some success criteria if your project structure does not support them. This is why it is important for both project managers and upper management to understand the benefits and challenges of the various project structures and set measures for success accordingly. If, for example, meeting deadlines is crucial for the organization, management should assign a Stand-Alone or Partnership Structure.

> **Take a Moment**
>
> Let's return to Sarah's neighborhood garden project from the beginning of the chapter.
>
> 1. What do you think are the Task Accomplishment success criteria that are most important for this project?
>
>    _____
>    _____
>    _____
>
> 2. What do you think are the Management System success criteria that are most important to this project?
>
>    _____
>    _____
>    _____
>
> 3. Based on your decisions above, which of the three project structure types—Appended, Partnership, or Stand-Alone—would you recommend to Sarah for her neighborhood garden project?
>
>    _____

What did you decide were the Task Accomplishment success criteria for Sarah's project? Meeting deadlines would certainly be critical because garden planting must occur sometime in May to reap a harvest in the fall. Creating change would also be important since the purpose of the project is to instill a sense of ownership and pride in the city.

As Management success measures, buy-in and closure would both be important in this project. The project will only work if Sarah can obtain the buy-in of the neighborhood associations,

# Measuring Project Success

and it will be necessary for the project to become part of an existing city government unit so that it becomes a regular summer activity in the neighborhoods.

In terms of project structure, the most effective would probably be Partnership: Partnership is the best structure to use to achieve buy-in and the kind of closure that would be desired for this project.

Although Stand-Alone is indicated for timeliness and change, Partnership is the second most desirable for each, and, with the necessity of working with the neighborhood associations, would work the best. Also, the project would not require the dedication of full-time project team members to get it accomplished on time. So, the indicators would lead to the selection of the Partnership structure.

## Choosing a Structure: A Case Study

Let's apply what we've learned so far about structuring a project to Leigh's situation, which was introduced in Chapter One. As you will recall, she has been asked to establish and then supervise a new customer service unit. This will involve:

- Recommending the number and type of staff needed.
- Creating the job descriptions.
- Setting up where the unit will work.
- Setting up the training.
- Determining the processes and systems that will need to be developed.
- Deciding how the unit will interact with the rest of the organization.

Leigh and her manager have decided that she will need the assistance of Human Resources, Facilities Management, Information Technology, Communications, Training and Organizational Development, and the Quality Team to complete the project.

Although the company Leigh works for is progressive and recognizes that it must improve its customer service to retain its market share, it is a small company without a lot of resources. It has accomplished impressive things with little additional money, and Leigh is told that the expectations will be similar for this project. Leigh just sees this as an additional challenge that does not diminish her excitement or cause her concern.

# Measuring Project Success

Leigh feels comfortable with her understanding of the intent of the project, its scope, and the outcomes it is to achieve. It is clear that the measures that will be used to determine whether or not the project is a success are implementing outcomes, creating change, gaining buy-in, and managing risk.

It is now time for Leigh to make her recommendation to her boss as to how the project should be structured.

> **Take a Moment**
>
> 1. What would be the best project structure for her to recommend and why?
>
>    _____
>
>    _____
>
> 2. What would be the least effective structure for Leigh to recommend and why?
>
>    _____
>
>    _____

Did you select Partnership as the best structure to recommend? Here are several reasons why this would be a good choice:

- Leigh and her manager determined that they will need the assistance of six other areas of the organization to get the new customer service unit up and operational. By organizing the team in the Partnership Structure, they can draw on those other areas for team members. If she chooses the Appended structure, these other areas of expertise will not be available to her.

- The company Leigh works with is small, without a lot of resources. This immediately eliminates the Stand-Alone Structure because it requires a lot of resources.

- The Partnership Structure will be the most effective in dealing with the success criteria of implementing outcomes and gaining buy-in and will be the second most effective for creating change and managing risk. These scores outweigh the effectiveness of either the Stand-Alone or the Appended Structures with these particular criteria.

What structure did you select as the least effective? Here are some reasons why you might have chosen Appended:

- Both the Stand-Alone and Partnership Structures would give Leigh the opportunity to include team members from the areas of the organization from which she and her manager identified she would need help.

- Although the Appended Structure ranks the highest in the risk management criteria, it ranks the least effective with all of the other identified success criteria.

## Chapter Summary

The organization and the project manager should determine how project success will be measured during the project's Inception Stage. There are two main sets of criteria for measuring project success:

- Whether project tasks are accomplished
- How the project is managed

Criteria dealing with the accomplishment of the tasks are:
- Meeting deadlines
- Implementing outcomes
- Maintaining customer confidence
- Creating change

Criteria dealing with the management of the project are:
- Gaining buy-in
- Providing access
- Managing risk
- Providing closure

Whether or not these criteria are met can be impacted by the type of project structure chosen.

# Measuring Project Success

## Self Check: Chapter Four Review

Answers to the following questions appear on page 129.

1. What are the two main sets of criteria for measuring project success?

    a. _____

    b. _____

2. Match each of the success criteria listed below with the project structure that best supports it.

    A = Appended Structure
    S = Stand-Alone Structure
    P = Partnership Structure

    _____ a. Meeting deadlines

    _____ b. Implementing outcomes

    _____ c. Maintaining customer confidence

    _____ d. Creating change

    _____ e. Gaining buy-in

    _____ f. Providing access

    _____ g. Managing risk

    _____ h. Providing closure

● **Selecting the Project Manager**

# Chapter *Five*
## *Selecting the Project Manager*

### Chapter Objectives

▶ Recognize the relationship among structural types, critical success criteria, and the project manager's roles and responsibilities.

▶ Understand the elements to be considered in staffing the project.

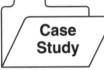
Case Study

Sharmaign has an important decision to make. Whom will she select to manage the upcoming project? Everyone is working at maximum capacity, so she cannot just pick someone who has the time to do it. And, because of the importance of the project to the organization, there are other criteria more important than available time to consider.

Sharmaign has selected Jerome, Nancy, and Gina as her three top candidates, but they are so different from each other, she needs to be more organized in her thinking to make the final selection.

Jerome is bright and ambitious and always seems to be on top of any assignment. He has the unique ability to formulate and see the vision, as well as get down to the detail to get it accomplished. He functions as a team leader in his current job and has helped Sharmaign with some management and personnel issues over the last year.

Jerome's coworkers like him, but he does not seem to be good at developing relationships with people outside his immediate area. He has enjoyed the limelight on those few occasions when a special assignment has gotten his name in the company newsletter or he has received public recognition at the company annual banquet.

## Selecting the Project Manager

Nancy is that steady, dependable, solid employee that every manager loves to have. She is organized and very good with detail. Sharmaign has used Nancy on several occasions to smooth over conflicts with other departments that have developed through some misunderstanding.

Nancy is a great communicator and has initiated several reporting processes within Sharmaign's department and between Sharmaign and other departments that work closely together. Nancy is the person that other employees seek out for advice with problems, personal as well as business related. Even though Nancy is comfortable with the status quo, she views change as a challenge and is flexible with handling new assignments.

Gina is very competent in her job, is great with detail, and, as with Jerome, can understand the vision. She can manage many responsibilities at one time and is one of the first people Sharmaign thinks of when assignments need to be delegated.

People like Gina, but she is very shy. She likes to work behind the scenes and is always promoting others to receive the public recognition that she should share in. She is comfortable with her coworkers in her own area, but not as comfortable with people from other departments. She can be the person "in charge," but this is not her preferred role.

We've considered a number of different project scenarios in previous chapters. What can we glean from them about what the project manager's job is and what skills she or he will need to be successful? Well, for one thing, no two projects are alike, even though they all go through the same stages.

**No two projects are alike.**

We can also see that projects are complex and vary in size, familiarity, and consequences. It is also clear that in each of these situations the project manager is the one who will provide focus and be accountable for the results or goals. But what do project managers need to know to succeed?

The structure of a project—Appended, Stand-Alone, or Partnership—makes a great difference in the degree of interface, influence, and conflict resolution skills needed by the project manager. Let's look at each of these structural types to see how they influence the skills needed by the project manager and the challenges they afford.

# Selecting the Project Manager

## Managing the Appended Project

As you'll recall, in this project structure neither the project manager nor the team members are relieved of any of their current duties and responsibilities, nor are specific percentages of their time allocated for project responsibilities. Essentially, the project assignment is added, or appended, to an already full workload.

> Within the Appended Structure, the project manager's role often consists of monitoring, obtaining information, and following up.

Actually labeling someone's role as a project manager within this type of structure may be a misnomer. It may be more accurate to call the person a project leader since the strategic management of the project is left to top management, and the project manager's role often consists of monitoring, obtaining information, and following up.

The leader of an Appended Project trades on the influence of the sponsoring executive. Much of the project leader's time may be spent prying the completion of project tasks out of staff members who consider them as lower level priorities in light of their "real" job responsibilities. Patience, persistence, knowing when to call on the authority of the project sponsor, and tracking and monitoring timelines and tasks will be critical in carrying out project leadership responsibilities in this type of structure.

If you look at project management as the opportunity to use your interpersonal and management skills in an environment that supports risk taking and visibility, an Appended Structure will not mesh well with your goals. On the other hand, if working with others in a reasonably controlled project environment fits with your personal needs, this may be the type of structure that will appeal to you and in which you will be successful.

## Managing the Stand-Alone Project

The Stand-Alone project may exist within the larger organizational context with some links to shared resources that project sponsors don't want to duplicate. Or the project may be totally on its own with the resources to acquire all that it needs. The project team members are removed from their areas of functional responsibility to devote 100 percent of their time to the project, including the full-time project manager.

# Selecting the Project Manager

A Stand-Alone project requires a project manager who can quickly meet the project's ever-changing needs while navigating the administrative details of hiring, firing, performance evaluation, scheduling, and budgeting. The project manager who manages in the Stand-Alone environment has to:

- Be clear about the project goals and remain focused on them.

- Stay current with the project schedule, plan, budget, and adjustments.

- Provide all necessary supervisory and human resources functions.

- Manage the communication interfaces needed to maintain project visibility and credibility.

## Managing the Partnership Project

In the partnership structure, the project team members spend a portion of their time working on the project and a portion of their time on their regular responsibilities. They report to both their regular supervisor and the project manager.

The Partnership Structure requires:

- Strong conflict management skills.

- Ability to manage the interfaces between the functional issues and project issues.

- Negotiation skills.

Project managers in this structure need to recognize that, although they certainly have a degree of authority, they do not have operating management authority over the team members. Instead, they must learn to effectively use the influence gained from the position of project manager.

If you are skilled in collaboratively working with conflicts, are comfortable dealing with ambiguity and ever-shifting resources, and have good communication skills, you will work well in a Partnership Structure.

### Selecting the Project Manager

On the other hand, if you need total control over staffing and do not enjoy gaining the commitment, cooperation, and support of other parts of the organization, you may not have the skills needed to be successful in a Partnership Structure.

Although all project management structures are valid, the perspective we will take in the rest of this chapter is that the project manager's job is most challenging in either a Stand-Alone or Partnership Structure. We will focus on what it takes to be successful in these structures, realizing that these skills and abilities can't help aiding those working in an Appended Structure.

### Take a Moment

Go back to the beginning of the chapter and reread Sharmaign's problem. What types of project do you think Jerome, Nancy, and Gina would be the most successful managing?

1. What type of project structure—Stand-Alone, Partnership, or Appended—would Jerome be the most successful with and why? What type would he be least successful with and why?

   _____

   _____

2. How about Nancy? In what project structure would she perform most successfully as a project manager? Why? In what project structure would she be least successful? Why?

   _____

   _____

   _____

   *continued on next page*

# Selecting the Project Manager

> **Take a Moment** *(continued)*
>
> 3. And finally, Gina. What would be the most successful and least successful project structures for her to manage and why?
>
> _____
>
> _____
>
> _____

Did you select the Stand-Alone Structure as the best suited for Jerome and the Partnership Structure as the least? Jerome is very organized, can easily handle a lot of different things simultaneously, and enjoys "being in charge," all characteristics that a Stand-Alone project manager must have. He also has some background in management and personnel issues. On the other hand, he is not a good relationship builder, an absolute must for someone to manage in a Partnership Structure.

Nancy would do well as a Partnership project manager. She is good at building relationships and is organized, flexible, and enjoys change. She is also oriented toward communication with others, which is extremely important when you are coordinating employees' work time with other supervisors. She does not have the management experience to be the only supervisor of a project team as in a Stand-Alone project, but does have the ability to jointly lead a team in conjunction with the members' operational supervisor.

Gina would do best in an Appended Structure and not very well in either of the others. She is too shy to take on the responsibility of the Stand-Alone or Partnership Structures. She is, however, organized, detailed, and can juggle many responsibilities at once, and would be very successful with the influence of her manager to lean on to help her get the job done.

### Selecting the Project Manager

## What a Project Manager Needs to Know

Unlike ongoing managers, the project manager doesn't need to worry about the overall operation of the organization. He or she is solely focused on the goals of the project for its duration. It's a narrower perspective, but one with considerable depth since project managers must deal with many of the same issues ongoing managers face (staffing, availability of equipment, planning, accountability for goals, etc.). Speed and access to resources are crucial.

> **Project managers frequently invent processes and procedures as they go.**

Project managers frequently invent processes and procedures as they go. They must constantly keep in touch with the key players and keep team members moving toward deadlines as resource issues arise.

To accomplish all of these tasks, project managers should keep the following guidelines in mind:

1. **Conflicts are inevitable.** If you aren't comfortable dealing with conflicts, project managing is not the place to be.

2. **Project management is not a job for someone who seeks the glory of recognition.** Most successful project managers know when to accept credit and when to be sure the credit is passed on to others on the team or within the larger organization. Although project managers are held accountable for project outcomes, they don't accomplish the results alone. As a project manager, strive to promote others more than yourself.

3. **All projects bring about change.** Whether that change affects a process, a product, relationships, or procedures, change is what projects are about. Some people welcome change, others are threatened by it, and others try to deny it. Recognizing that people deal differently with change will help you understand responses to your project.

4. **Things will go wrong.** If your goal is perfection, you will fail. Project managers are measured not on their ability to avoid mistakes, but on how they handle them when they occur. If you take the organizational approaches we have described in previous chapters, you will minimize many of

the problems that could occur. Many of the other issues that surface during plan development and implementation can be effectively dealt with by remembering to manage your communications with key players and staff up, down, and around the organization.

5. **As project manager, you must make things happen.** The project relies on you for leadership. Your influence skills, your leveraging of the authority of the sponsor(s), and your political savvy will all make or break the project.

## Staffing the Project

In many organizations, the project manager decides or helps decide who should become members of the project team. Good team members are critical to the success of your project. The following list of characteristics will help you as you make your selections:

> Good team members are critical to the success of your project.

### Communication Skills

Team members should have skill in both written and oral communication. A project team does not need someone who never shares information. Communication is one of the biggest problems in any organization and can be a special problem within a project team. The entire team needs to know what is going on—especially the project manager.

### Relationship-Building Skills

Projects are not done in a vacuum. A project team often needs input and assistance from people outside the team. This will be much easier to obtain if team members build and maintain constructive relationships. Good working relationships must also be developed within the team. Strong team relationships will help create a successful project outcome.

### Ability to Work on a Team

Project team members cannot be loners. Team members must feel that they can depend on each other. Trust is very important for the successful outcome of the project.

● **Selecting the Project Manager**

### Flexibility

It is important for team members to feel comfortable with sharing their opinions and views. However, it is not possible for team members always to have things their own way. They must be able to be comfortable with consensus or being told how it will be.

### Openness to Change

There will be lots of changes as the project moves along. Change can happen fast without much planning. And usually the result of the completion of a project is change. Team members who are not comfortable with change can become roadblocks to project completion.

> Team members who are not comfortable with change can become roadblocks to project completion.

### Comfort with the Project Structure

- Appended: Team members must be organized enough to add additional responsibility to their regular work.

- Partnership: Team members must be organized enough to add additional responsibility and additional work. And they must be comfortable with two bosses, their functional boss and the project manager.

- Stand-Alone: Team members may be required to be risk takers regarding project success and future job opportunities.

### Technical Knowledge

Technical requirements of the project must be met in order for it to be successfully completed.

## Chapter Summary

In this chapter, we discussed the characteristics of the successful project manager for each of the three project structures.

- In the Appended Structure, the project manager should be patient and persistent, know when to call on the authority of the supervising manager, and know how to track and monitor timelines and tasks.

- In the Stand-Alone Structure, the project manager must be organized, communicate well, manage time well, feel comfortable with authority, have good supervisory skills, enjoy visibility, and enjoy working in a fast-paced environment.

- In a Partnership Structure, the project manager must be both flexible and organized, negotiate and resolve conflict well, build relationships, and not mind not being "in charge."

There are five things that any project manager must recognize:

1. Conflict is inevitable.
2. Project management is not the job for glory seekers.
3. Projects result in change.
4. Things will go wrong.
5. You must make things happen.

Choosing the project team is critical to the project's success. Some characteristics essential in all staff include:

- Communication skills.
- Relationship-building skills.
- Ability to work on a team.
- Flexibility.
- Openness to change.
- Comfort with the project structure.
- Technical knowledge.

## Selecting the Project Manager

### Self Check: Chapter Five Review

Answers to the following questions appear on page 130.

Match the characteristics of the successful project manager to the correct structure.

A. The Appended Structure
B. The Stand-Alone Structure
C. The Partnership Structure

___ 1. In this structure, the project manager must be organized, communicate well, manage time well, feel comfortable with authority, have good supervisory skills, enjoy visibility, and enjoy working in a fast-paced environment.

___ 2. In this structure, the project manager must be flexible and organized, negotiate and resolve conflict well, build relationships, and not mind not being in charge.

___ 3. In this structure, the project manager must be patient and persistent, know when to call on the authority of the supervising manager, and know how to track and monitor timelines and tasks.

4. List three characteristics that are important for all project team members:

   a. _____

   b. _____

   c. _____

## Selecting the Project Manager

**Notes**

# Stage 2: Start-Up

Stage 2, the Start-Up Stage, should take about as long as the Inception Stage. This stage builds on the Stage 1 foundation by:

1. Creating the project plan
2. Setting the project budget

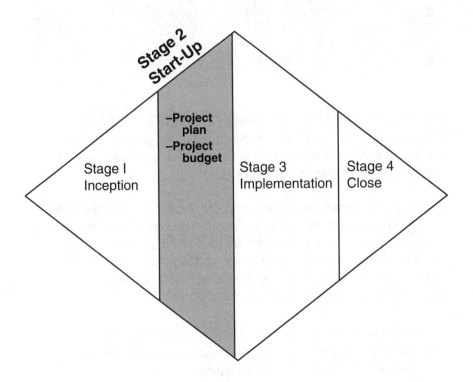

● Planning the Project

# Chapter Six

## Planning the Project

### Chapter Objectives

▶ Create a Work Breakdown Structure and a Network Diagram.

▶ Calculate the time it will take to finish the project.

▶ Develop a project timeline using a GANTT chart format.

▶ Set the project budget.

**Case Study**

Remember Leigh from Chapters One and Four? She is beginning her work as the manager of the project to set up a new customer service unit. The project has been named "Project VIC" for Very Important Customer.

Leigh has selected her team members, and they are now looking to her for direction on how to proceed. She has a lot of things that she knows will need to be done as part of the project, but she is having difficulty putting some order and logic to them. What should she do? Where should she start? And how will she then keep track of the project's progress?

There are ten steps to successfully planning a project:
1. Identify the tasks/activities needed to accomplish the project (Work Breakdown Structure).
2. Determine the relationship among the tasks.
3. Create a network diagram of tasks.
4. Estimate the optimistic, most likely, and pessimistic completion time for each task.
5. Using the three times determined in Step 4, calculate the expected time for each task.
6. Calculate the time for completing each path on the network diagram.

# Planning the Project

7. Identify the critical path.
8. Calculate the slack.
9. Establish the timeline.
10. Set the project budget.

In this chapter, we will discuss each of these steps and apply them to Leigh's project to help her develop her project plan.

## Step 1: Identifying the Work Breakdown Structure

Begin to organize a project by identifying all the tasks that must be done to complete it. Any project, whether big or small, can seem overwhelming at first glance. A good approach is to break the project into its smallest component parts. Each small part can then be dealt with on its own in the order in which it needs to occur, and the work becomes less overwhelming.

> **Begin to organize a project by identifying all the tasks that must be done to complete it.**

Ask the project team for help breaking the project down into its component parts. Hold a brainstorming session with all the team members to identify what tasks need to be accomplished to finish the project. There are four general rules to follow when brainstorming:

- No team member can criticize or judge another's idea until all ideas are on the table.

- Think "out of the box." The wilder the idea, the better.

- Seek quantity rather than quality. The more ideas generated, the higher the likelihood that several will be usable.

- Once all ideas have been exhausted, combine and improve on them. How can the ideas of others be turned into better ideas, or how can two or more ideas be joined into still another idea?

## Planning the Project

Let's look in on Leigh and see how her team has done with their brainstorming session.

Leigh's team has covered the wall of the conference room with sheets of chart paper filled with ideas, and these have been consolidated into the project tasks. A partial list of these tasks looks like this:

- ✓ Decide what the customer service unit will do.
- ✓ Write job descriptions.
- ✓ Create the organizational chart for the unit.
- ✓ Analyze the potential workload.
- ✓ Determine space needs within the unit.
- ✓ Determine work/information flow with other units.
- ✓ Order furniture.
- ✓ Set up offices after furniture delivery.
- ✓ Order phones.
- ✓ Supervise phone installation.
- ✓ Identify information customer service workers will need to do their jobs.
- ✓ Identify information available on the network.
- ✓ Identify information from other sources.
- ✓ Work with Information Technology so information needs are met.
- ✓ Develop training for customer service representatives.
- ✓ Develop training for other units interfacing with customer service unit.
- ✓ Train unit employees.
- ✓ Train other interfacing units.
- ✓ Hire new staff.
- ✓ Determine work flow within the unit.

# Planning the Project

> ## Take a Moment
> To get a feel for the mental process one uses in generating a list of tasks, consider the problem of rearranging the space that your unit is in. Quickly list six to 10 things that would have to be done in order to get this accomplished. Don't put them in any order—just jot them down as they come to you.
>
> _____   _____
>
> _____   _____
>
> _____   _____
>
> _____   _____
>
> _____   _____

How creative did you let yourself be? Were you critical and judgmental, or did you just let the ideas flow, knowing that they would be evaluated later?

## Organizing the Tasks

Once the project tasks are identified, they must be organized into logical groupings. This is called developing the Work Breakdown Structure. The Work Breakdown Structure, or WBS, then becomes the basis for assigning responsibilities to the team members; establishing costs and budgets; tracking time, costs, and performance; and status reporting.

> **Once the project tasks are identified, they must be organized into logical groupings.**

There are many ways that the tasks can be logically grouped:

- By the major players who are on the team or involved in a substantial way in the completion of the project

- By the organizational units represented on the team or that will be impacted in some way by the project

- By functional units within the organization that will be involved or impacted by the project

- By vendors if the project has major components delivered by suppliers

# Planning the Project

- By location if there are various facilities involved
- By the chronological order in which they must be completed
- By logical/functional task relationships unique to the project

There are probably many other organizational patterns you can identify for a specific project. What is important in developing the WBS is that it be organized in a way that makes sense for the type of project and the project environment as well as what the project manager is comfortable with.

Let's look at the tasks that were identified by Leigh's project team.

**Case Study**

### Tasks Identified by Leigh's Team
**Work**
- ✓ Analyze the potential workload.
- ✓ Determine work/information flow with other units.
- ✓ Identify information unit workers will need.
- ✓ Determine work flow within the unit.
- ✓ Work with Information Technology so information needs are met.
- ✓ Identify information available on the network.
- ✓ Decide what the customer service unit will do.

**Personnel**
- ✓ Train other interfacing units.
- ✓ Create organizational chart—how the unit will look, number of employees.
- ✓ Hire new staff.
- ✓ Develop training for other units interfacing with customer service unit.
- ✓ Train unit employees.
- ✓ Develop training for customer service representatives.
- ✓ Write job descriptions.

**Facility**
- ✓ Set up furniture.
- ✓ Phone installation.
- ✓ Order furniture.
- ✓ Order phones.
- ✓ Determine space needs within the unit.

# Planning the Project

Leigh selected logical functional task relationships. As the manager of this same project, you might have done it differently. There is no right or wrong way to organize the tasks, just as long as some form of organization is accomplished and you, as the project manager, feel comfortable with it.

## Take a Moment

Return to our previous exercise and the list of tasks that would be required to rearrange your unit's work space. Using the example above as a guide, determine the best way to organize them, and write your organizational scheme below.

_____    _____

_____    _____

_____    _____

_____    _____

_____

What was your reason for organizing them the way that you did? Is there another way that you could also have organized them? What is it?

_____

_____

## Step 2: Determining Task Relationships

The next step in organizing a project is to determine the task sequence and dependency. A task is dependent on another task if it cannot be started until the first task is completed. An easy way to organize project tasks is to write each task on a Post-it® Note. Then place the last task of each of the organizational groupings on a wall or a board and work backward. On the following page you can see how Leigh's team arranged their tasks.

## Planning the Project

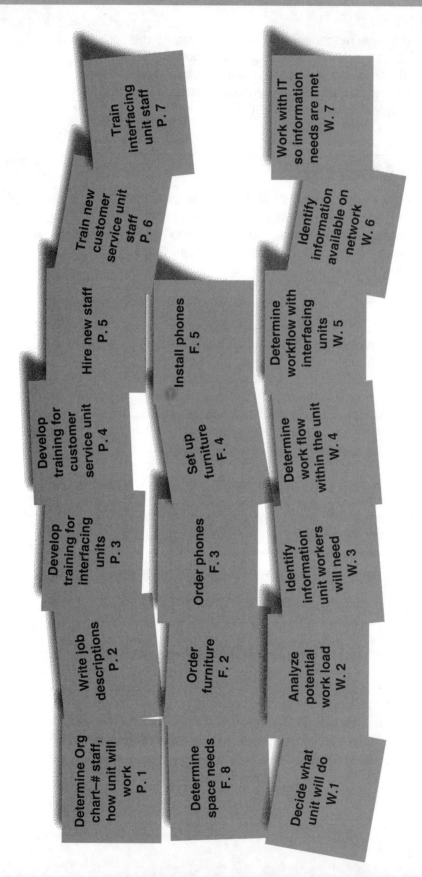

**Post-it® Notes—Arrangement 1**
(numbers are assigned based on category identification and sequence)

# Planning the Project

The numbers assigned to each of the tasks in the WBS can be used as a shorthand way of referring to tasks when assigning responsibilities to team members; establishing costs and budgets; tracking time, costs, and performance; and status reporting.

> ## Take a Moment
>
> Transfer the tasks you identified for the project to rearrange your work unit's space to Post-it® Notes. Then, beginning with the last task in each of your logical groupings, place them in sequential order working backwards and assign a number to each.
>
> You now have completed a WBS for rearranging your work unit's space. The benefits of going through this process are that it can be used for such things as assigning team responsibilities, calculating costs and budgets, monitoring task completion, and preparing project status reports. It can also help you avoid missing any crucial tasks that could jeopardize the successful completion of the project.

## Step 3: Creating the Network Diagram

The next step in the process of planning a project is the creation of the network diagram. Leigh's team is now ready to use the work breakdown structure to create a network diagram for their project. They begin by looking at the interdependency of the tasks and reorganizing the Post-It® notes based on this. Remember that we said that a task is dependent on another task if it cannot be started until the first task in completed. Here is the result of their work. Notice that the chronological sequence of the task is kept pretty much intact, but the original organization of the task into functional areas has become less apparent, and less important.

## Planning the Project

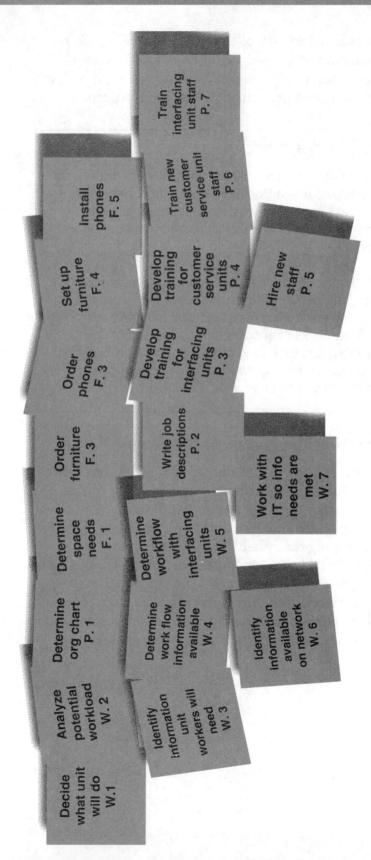

Post-It® Notes—Arrangement 2

# Planning the Project

We are now able to see which tasks are dependent on each other (for example W.1 must be completed before W.2 and W.3; W.3 must be completed before W.4 and W.6). The next step is to put the tasks into the network diagram format.

## Activities and Events

There are two components of a Network Diagram: activities and events.

An activity:

- Is one of the tasks that we have identified for our project.
- Has a definite start and stop point.
- Has a starting event and a stopping event.
- Is described by the numbers assigned to each event.
- Is represented on the Network Diagram by an arrow pointing in the direction of the time flow of the project.

An event:

- Signals the starting or ending of an activity.
- Occurs when all activities pointing into it have been completed.
- Is represented by a circle on the Network Diagram. Each circle has a unique number. The first event on the left side of the diagram could be a one or a ten, for example. Numbering by fives or tens allows the insertion of additional activities and events without renumbering the entire diagram as the project moves along and more tasks are identified. The numbering of the events should occur as the last thing to complete the network diagram.

*Burst events* represent two or more activities starting at the same time. *Merge events* represent two or more activities ending at the same time.

> There are two components of a Network Diagram: activities and events.

● **Planning the Project**

## Activities/Events Example

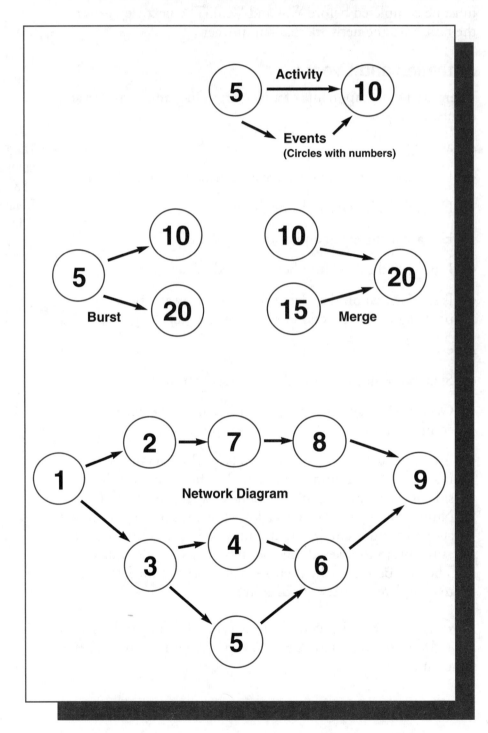

# Planning the Project

Use the following basic rules for creating a network diagram.

## Basic Rules

- All events are uniquely numbered.

- Starting event numbers must be smaller than ending event numbers.

- All activities must have a unique pair of event numbers.

- All diagrams should have only one starting event at the beginning of the network and only one ending event at the end of the network.

A caution when developing and then using a network diagram for managing the project: there is no relationship between the length of the arrow and the time required to finish an activity. A network diagram illustrates sequence and dependency, not time.

Creating a network diagram was an especially good exercise for Leigh's team because it gave them a good sense of the overall project as well as an appreciation of the importance of completing certain tasks before others could be started. The network diagram they created for the list of tasks that we have been using appears on the next page.

Case Study

# Planning the Project

## Network Diagram #1

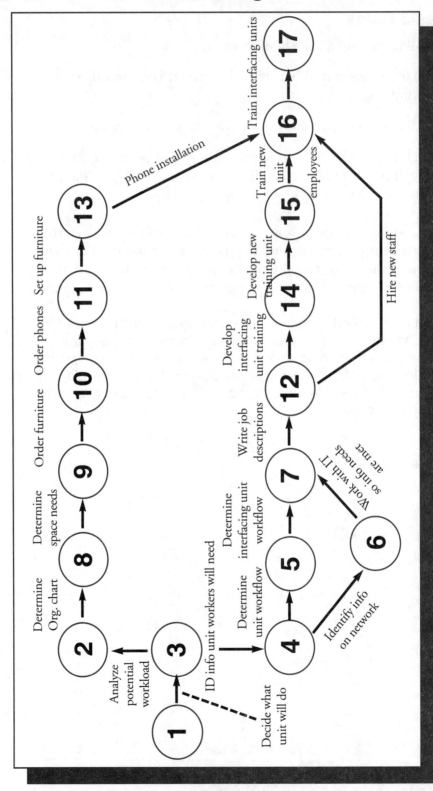

# Planning the Project

There is no right or wrong network diagram for a particular project. You may look at the sequence of tasks on the previous page and feel that one or more should be changed or rearranged. What is important is that the team takes the time to plan out the project. The success of a project is determined in large part by the quality of the planning done before it is begun.

> **Take a Moment**
>
> Apply the basic rules above for creating a network diagram for the WBS that you have created for the rearrangement of your work unit's area and create your own network diagram.
>
> Was this an easy exercise for you? Are you clear on the difference between an activity and an event? Do you understand the benefit of creating this diagram before beginning the actual project tasks?

## Step 4: Estimating Time Needed

Some projects are repetitive—they have been done many times in the past and will be done many times in the future. Construction projects would be an example of these repetitive projects. When you build a garage, there are certain tasks that always need to be done, they are always done in the same order, and they always take about the same amount of time to complete. Estimating time in these projects is not a major issue.

However, you may be involved with a project that is being done for the first time and may never be repeated. You have no history to help you arrive at a good estimate of the time that it will take to do a particular task. But it is critical that the expected time that you use be as good an estimate as is humanly possible. Bringing a project in on time by the expected completion date will make or break your success as the project's manager. For these projects, it is recommended that you as the project manager consider three estimates of time for each task.

## Planning the Project

**Optimistic Time (TO)**—The shortest conceivable time for a task to be completed

- Assumes everything will go right
- Allows no delays in completing the task

**Pessimistic Time (TP)**—Best guess for the maximum time for a task to be completed

- Takes into account the normal delays that can be expected
- Does not consider any catastrophes

**Most Likely Time (TM)**—Best guess of the time for a task to be completed considering normal foul-ups and lucky breaks

- Is not figured as an average of TO and TP

## Step 5: Calculating the Expected Time

Once you have established the three estimates of time for each activity, you can calculate the expected time necessary for completing the task by applying the following formula:

$$\text{Expected Time (TE)} = \frac{TO + 4TM + TP}{6}$$

For example, let's say that we have a project task for which we have estimated the TO, TM, and TP as follows:

TO = 2
TM = 5
TP = 12

Applying these figures to the formula, we get:

$$\text{Expected time (TE)} = \frac{2 + (4 \times 5) + 12}{6}$$

$$= \frac{34}{6} = 5.6$$

## Planning the Project

Leigh's team determined the three estimated times for each of the activities and calculated the expected time for each. They are presented in the following table in days:

**Case Study**

| Activity | TO | TM | TP | TE |
|---|---|---|---|---|
| 2→8 | 1 | 3 | 5 | 3 |
| 7→12 | 7 | 10 | 15 | 10.3 |
| 12→14 | 20 | 30 | 35 | 29.2 |
| 14→15 | 20 | 30 | 35 | 29.2 |
| 12→16 | 20 | 30 | 40 | 33.3 |
| 15→16 | 2 | 3 | 5 | 3.2 |
| 16→17 | 2 | 3 | 5 | 3.2 |
| 8→9 | 3 | 5 | 10 | 5.5 |
| 9→10 | 5 | 10 | 15 | 10 |
| 10→11 | 2 | 3 | 4 | 3 |
| 11→13 | 4 | 7 | 10 | 7.7 |
| 13→16 | 5 | 10 | 15 | 10 |
| 1→3 | 5 | 10 | 15 | 10 |
| 3→2 | 6 | 12 | 17 | 11.8 |
| 3→4 | 20 | 27 | 33 | 26.8 |
| 4→5 | 3 | 7 | 12 | 7.2 |
| 5→7 | 3 | 7 | 11 | 7 |
| 4→6 | 5 | 7 | 10 | 8 |
| 6→7 | 45 | 75 | 100 | 74.2 |

● **Planning the Project**

## Step 6: Calculating the Time for Each Path

A path is the way that one could start at the beginning of the diagram and go to the end by following events and activities.

Leigh's team placed the estimated times on their network diagram and calculated the time required to complete each of the paths. How many paths are there in Network Diagram 1? Do you see that there are five? The paths and their associated times are:

| PATH A | Expected Time | | PATH B | Expected Time |
|---|---|---|---|---|
| 1→3 | 10.0 | | 1→3 | 10.0 |
| 3→2 | 11.8 | | 3→4 | 26.8 |
| 2→8 | 3.0 | | 4→5 | 7.2 |
| 8→9 | 5.5 | | 5→7 | 7.0 |
| 9→10 | 10.0 | | 7→12 | 10.3 |
| 10→11 | 3.0 | | 12→14 | 29.2 |
| 11→13 | 7.7 | | 14→15 | 29.2 |
| 13→16 | 10.0 | | 15→16 | 3.2 |
| 16→17 | 3.2 | | 16→17 | 3.2 |
| Path A TE | 64.2 days | | Path B TE | 126.1 days |

| PATH C | Expected Time | | PATH D | Expected Time |
|---|---|---|---|---|
| 1→3 | 10.0 | | 1→3 | 10.0 |
| 3→4 | 26.8 | | 3→4 | 26.8 |
| 4→6 | 8.0 | | 4→5 | 7.2 |
| 6→7 | 74.2 | | 5→7 | 7.0 |
| 7→12 | 10.3 | | 7→12 | 10.3 |
| 12→14 | 29.2 | | 12→16 | 33.3 |
| 14→15 | 29.2 | | 16→17 | 3.2 |
| 15→16 | 3.2 | | Path D TE | 97.8 days |
| 16→17 | 3.2 | | | |
| Path C TE | 194.1 days | | | |

| PATH E | Expected Time |
|---|---|
| 1→3 | 10.0 |
| 3→4 | 26.8 |
| 4→6 | 8.0 |
| 6→7 | 74.2 |
| 7→12 | 10.3 |
| 12→16 | 33.3 |
| 16→17 | 3.2 |
| Path E TE | 165.8 days |

## Step 7: Identifying the Critical Path

From these calculations, it is now possible to determine which of the paths is the *critical path*. *The critical path is the path in the Network Diagram that requires the greatest amount of time to complete.* It is, in other words, the longest path. For Leigh's project, the critical path is Path C, which team members have estimated will take 194.1 days to complete. Path C, the critical path, is identified by the dark arrows in Network Diagram 2.

## Planning the Project

## Network Diagram #2

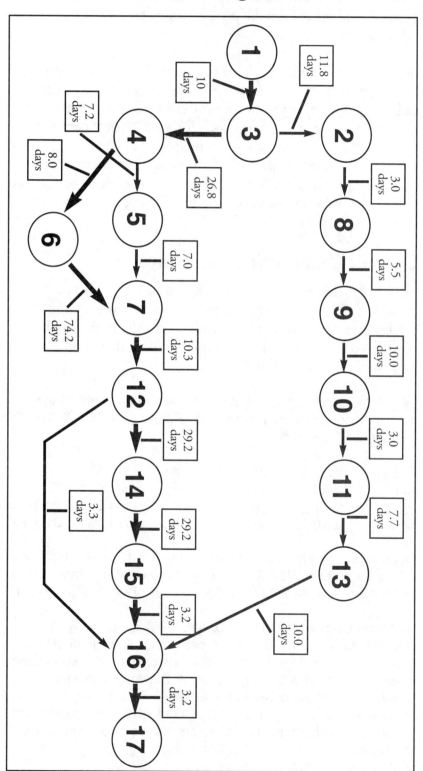

# ● Planning the Project

Why is it important to know the critical path of the project plan? Why are these tasks more critical than any others in the project? And what does the project manager do with this information?

Because the tasks on the critical path take the longest to complete, any delay in any of these will delay the project. Delay in other tasks may not affect the entire project in this way, depending on the length of the delay. The tasks along the critical path are those that the project manager must pay the greatest amount of attention to in terms of completion date. The others are, of course, important, but not as important to get done by the due date as the tasks on the critical path. This is because the other paths contain slack.

> *Slack* is the difference between the time requirements of the critical path and the others on the network.

## Step 8: Calculating the Slack

*Slack* is the difference between the time requirements of the critical path and the others on the network. It is the time available to be "played around with" and still get that path completed by the estimated completion date that is not available on the critical path.

**Case Study**

Leigh's team calculated the slack for each of the paths of their network diagram by subtracting the TE for a specific path from the TE for the critical path.

| Path A | Path B | Path D | Path E | |
|---|---|---|---|---|
| 194.1 | 194.1 | 194.1 | 194.1 | Critical Path TE |
| 64.2 | 126.1 | 97.8 | 165.8 | Less Other Path TE |
| 129.9 | 68.0 | 96.3 | 28.3 | Slack Within Other Path |

Leigh and her team now know that there are 129.9 days of slack within the tasks on Path A, 68.0 days of slack within Path B, 96.3 days of slack within Path D, and 28.3 days of slack within Path E.

What can Leigh do with this information? She can delay the planned starting of tasks within these paths. She can divert resources planned for these paths to the critical path, shortening it—and the length of the entire project. She knows that team members assigned to tasks on the paths with slack will have some free that can be used for things outside of the project. Can you think of other things that a project manager can do with this information?

## Planning the Project

### Take a Moment

We have now completed seven of the nine steps in creating the project plan. Before we move on to the last two, let's apply what you've learned to your project of rearranging your work unit's area.

1. Identify the Optimistic (TO), Most Likely (TM), and Pessimistic (TP) times for each of the activities on your network diagram.

   _____  _____  _____

2. Calculate the Expected Time (TE) for each activity using the formula.

   $$TE = \frac{TO + 4TM + TP}{6}$$

   _____

3. Determine the number of paths on your network and calculate the Expected Time (TE) for each path.

   _____

4. Identify the critical path.

   _____

5. Calculate the slack contained within the other, non-critical paths.

   _____

What will you do with the slack contained within the non-critical paths?

● **Planning the Project**

## Step 9: Establishing the Timeline

The network diagram illustrates the relationship of the tasks to one another and the sequence in which they should be done. It does not, however, show the tasks in relation to a timeline. A good way of doing this is to use a GANTT chart format.

On the following page is an example of a GANTT chart showing just the tasks on the critical path in Leigh's project. The chart that the project team would make and use would include all of the tasks of the project.

# Planning the Project

## GANTT Chart

| Task Name | November | | | | December | | | | | January | | | | February | | | | March | | | | April | | | | May | | | | June | | | | July | | | | August | | |
|---|---|---|---|---|---|---|---|---|---|---|---|---|---|---|---|---|---|---|---|---|---|---|---|---|---|---|---|---|---|---|---|---|---|---|---|---|---|---|---|---|
| | 1 | 2 | 3 | 4 | 1 | 2 | 3 | 4 | 5 | 1 | 2 | 3 | 4 | 1 | 2 | 3 | 4 | 1 | 2 | 3 | 4 | 1 | 2 | 3 | 4 | 1 | 2 | 3 | 4 | 1 | 2 | 3 | 4 | 1 | 2 | 3 | 4 | 1 | 2 | 3 |
| W. 1 Decide what CSU will do | ■ | | | | | | | | | | | | | | | | | | | | | | | | | | | | | | | | | | | | | | | |
| W. 3 ID info CSU will need | | | ■ | ■ | ■ | | | | | | | | | | | | | | | | | | | | | | | | | | | | | | | | | | | |
| W. 6 ID info available on network | | | | | | | ■ | ■ | | | | | | | | | | | | | | | | | | | | | | | | | | | | | | | | |
| W. 7 Work with IT so unit needs met | | | | | | | | | ■ | ■ | ■ | ■ | ■ | ■ | ■ | ■ | ■ | ■ | ■ | ■ | ■ | ■ | | | | | | | | | | | | | | | | | | |
| P. 2 Write job descriptions | | | | | | | | | | | | | | | | | | | | | | | | | ■ | | | | | | | | | | | | | | | |
| P. 3 Develop interfacing units training | | | | | | | | | | | | | | | | | | | | | | | | | | | ■ | ■ | ■ | ■ | | | | | | | | | | |
| P. 4 Develop CSU training | | | | | | | | | | | | | | | | | | | | | | | | | | | | | | | | ■ | ■ | ■ | ■ | ■ | | | | |
| P. 6 Train CSU staff | | | | | | | | | | | | | | | | | | | | | | | | | | | | | | | | | | | | | ■ | ■ | | |
| P.7 Train interfacing units | | | | | | | | | | | | | | | | | | | | | | | | | | | | | | | | | | | | | | | | ■ |

### ● Planning the Project

Notice that the project team took the tasks from the WBS and that their placement is a result of the Network Diagram, in regard both to the sequence in which tasks will be completed and the duration of the tasks. If we know when the project is to begin and the duration of the tasks, the dates that each of the tasks begins and ends is not difficult to determine.

GANTT charts are very useful as communication tools in showing the variances (if there are any) in completing a task from the planned completion. It is an easy tool for management, customers, and other groups interested in the status of the project to understand. It is also very easy to make, requiring just some graph paper, a pencil, and a ruler. There is also commercial software on the market that will make GANTT charts automatically. The weakness of a GANTT chart is that it does not easily convey the status of the entire project, just that of the individual tasks. And it does not indicate the interrelatedness of the tasks. The network diagram more easily illustrates both of these.

### Take a Moment

We are now finished with the steps to planning a successful project. Take a few minutes now and create a GANTT chart for your project of rearranging your work unit's area.

### Step 10: Setting the Project Budget

Once the tasks have been identified, the network diagram created, and the times for each task calculated, the budgeting for the project can begin.

What are some typical budget areas for any project?

- Personnel (salary and benefits)
- Equipment (purchase, lease or rental costs for copiers, telephones, desks, etc.)
- Supplies (like paper, pencils, staplers, etc.)
- Facilities (if rental of the team space is appropriate)
- Technology (personal computers, networking, Internet access, etc.)

# Planning the Project

Using the WBS and the network diagram, staff assignments can be made and equipment, supply, and technology needs identified. Use the organization numbers of the WBS to help track the project budget.

Once you've completed the project plan and set the budget, you're ready to move into the next project stage: Implementation.

## Chapter Summary

There are ten steps to successfully developing a project plan:

1. Identify and logically group the project tasks by developing the Work Breakdown Structure.

2. Create a Network Diagram showing the sequence and dependent relationships of tasks. Network Diagrams are made up of activities (designated by arrows) and events (designated by circles).

4. Build in the time considerations of optimistic (TO), most likely (TM), and pessimistic (TP) times.

5. Calculate the Expected Time for each task using the formula

$$TE = \frac{TO + 4TM + TP}{6}$$

6. Calculate the time for each path on the network diagram.

7. Determine the longest path, which is the critical path.

8. Calculate the slack contained in the noncritical paths.

9. Develop a GANTT chart. A GANTT chart is a good way to put the tasks of a project on a timeline and communicate the variance of the completion of tasks with their planned completion to your management or other interested groups. It is easy to make and understand. However, it does not show the interrelatedness of the tasks or give a true picture of the overall status of the project.

10. Once these tasks have been completed, it is possible to do the budgeting. Typical items to consider in budgeting include personnel costs, equipment, supplies, facilities, and technology.

● **Planning the Project**

### Self Check: Chapter Six Review

Answers appear on page 130.

Match the terms and definitions below.

\_\_\_ 1. First step in organizing a project
\_\_\_ 2. The Work Breakdown Structure
\_\_\_ 3. An activity
\_\_\_ 4. An event
\_\_\_ 5. The critical path
\_\_\_ 6. Slack

\_\_\_ A. The path in the Network Diagram that requires the most time to complete.
\_\_\_ B. Represented on the Network Diagram by an arrow pointing in the direction of the time flow of the project.
\_\_\_ C. The difference between the time requirements of the critical path and the others on the network.
\_\_\_ D. Organizing the project tasks into logical groups.
\_\_\_ E. Represented on the Network Diagram by a circle.
\_\_\_ F. Identifying all the tasks that must be done to complete the project.

7. What is the formula used to calculate the Expected Time for a task?

   _____

8. What is a good tool for putting the project tasks on a timeline and communicating project tasks to management?

   _____

   _____

**Planning the Project**

**Notes**

Notes

# Stage 3: Implementation

Stage 3, the Implementation Stage, is the longest stage of the project. In the Implementation Stage, the project manager's ability to manage multiple tasks, people issues, and organizational interfaces is challenged. Fast turnaround and consistent monitoring are critical to project success.

Tasks to be accomplished during this stage include:

1. Monitoring progress
2. Redesigning the project plan
3. Rescheduling dates
4. Reallocating resources
5. Delegating tasks
6. Resolving conflicts
7. Managing interfaces

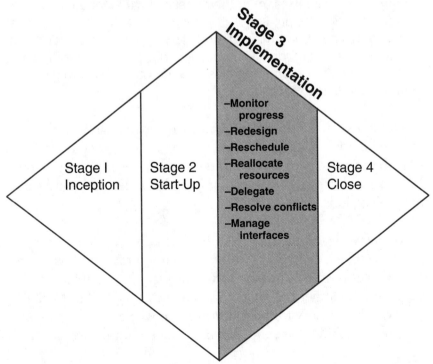

**Project Stage Model**
**Stage 3: Implementation**

• **Putting the Plan into Action**

# Chapter *Seven*
## *Putting the Plan into Action*

> **Chapter Objectives**
> ▶ Understand the project manager's tasks and tools for the implementation stage.
>
> ▶ Be aware of the project manager's responsibilities for resolving conflicts and managing project interfaces.

**Case Study**

Cory is a project manager with a problem. He and his team did a solid job of planning their project, so everyone assumed implementation would be a breeze. Unfortunately, the project team did not have all the information that was needed and available to develop the plan, and now some elements must be redesigned to add several key pieces.

Cory has not coped well with these needed changes and has not managed to keep the team or their bosses in the loop and aware of problems with the project. As a consequence, many of the initial target dates have been missed, and Cory is pressing for additional time from team members. Their bosses, however, are feeling the press of their other responsibilities and are not inclined to give more time to this project.

**The Implementation Stage will probably take the longest amount of time to complete.**

As you can see from the Project Stage Model on page 103, the Implementation Stage will probably take the longest amount of time to complete as compared to the other stages. This stage, after all, is when the team actually completes the project tasks and gets the project done.

All of the work and planning that has been done to date by the project team has been done with the intention that this stage go as smoothly as possible. And the better the planning in the first two stages, the smoother the project will go in this stage. But it will not go perfectly. As Cory found out, it is not possible to anticipate or control everything that can happen during the Implementation Stage.

## Putting the Plan into Action

Implementation is when the project manager begins to manage the project. This is accomplished through various tasks or activities: monitoring, rescheduling, redesigning, reallocating resources, delegating, resolving conflicts, and managing interfaces.

## Monitoring Progress

If you will recall from Chapter Six, the last thing that we did in completing the project plan was to schedule the tasks along a timeline using a GANTT Chart. The GANTT Chart should show the calendar date that tasks are to be started and completed, who will be working on those tasks, and, as the implementation moves along, if tasks are on, ahead of, or behind schedule.

The GANTT chart can then be used by the project manager and team members to monitor the project and to communicate to the other people within the company who need to know about the project. This could include sharing the status of individual tasks, when team members will be needed, when nonteam member assistance or other resources will be required, and many other pieces of information that will help other departments in their planning and keep the project on schedule.

So a major task of the project manager during implementation is to keep the GANTT Chart updated and to distribute it regularly to team members and interested parties in the company. The project manager also needs to analyze and use the information on the chart to identify, keep on top of, and minimize problems with implementation as quickly as possible. This kind of monitoring is the jumping off point for knowing when to carry out the other tasks and activities of this stage: redesigning, rescheduling, reallocating resources, delegating, resolving conflicts, and managing interfaces.

> **Implementation is when the project manager begins to manage the project.**

# ● Putting the Plan into Action

> ### Take a Moment
> Let's look at the situation that Cory is in from the scenario at the beginning of the chapter. Has he effectively used a tool like the GANTT chart to monitor the project? How do you know?
>
> _____
>
> _____
>
> _____

If Cory had been closely monitoring the project and regularly communicating the status of task completion to his team and their bosses, he could have taken corrective action at the first sign of problems, and he would not now be pressing team members and their bosses for additional time on the project.

## Redesigning the Project Plan

No matter how well a project manager sets up and plans a project, many unexpected things can happen during the Implementation Stage. The project plan completed during the Start-Up Stage is just that, a plan. The project manager must be flexible in his or her management style and willing to redesign the project plan if it becomes necessary.

*The project manager must be flexible in his or her management style.*

What could cause the project plan to be redesigned? An outcome identified during the Inception Phase is eliminated, or a new outcome is added. The project has fallen so far behind schedule that a new approach to completing it must be undertaken to get it done by the original due date. Or costs have skyrocketed and they must be brought under control to meet the original budget. These are just some examples, but all suggest a need to redesign the plan.

And how is the plan redesigned? If the tasks are affected, it will mean going back to the Work Breakdown Structure and working through the network diagram, the time, and the critical path and then preparing a new GANTT chart. If it is merely a rearrangement of the same tasks, this will affect the network diagram, the critical path, and GANTT chart. It may be that only assigned times for certain tasks are changed (more resources are available). This may impact the critical path and will impact the GANTT chart.

Often there is not a systematic review of the plan if a redesign is required because of the time pressures the project manager feels during the Implementation Stage. This is a mistake and will add to the potential for more and bigger problems down the way. The chances for project failure will be greatly increased.

> ### Take a Moment
> Let's look again at Cory's situation from the beginning scenario. If you were Cory, would you consider redesigning? What aspects of the plan would be affected?
>
> _____
> _____
> _____
> _____

Because the scenario mentions that key pieces will have to be added to the plan, we can assume that new tasks will be added. This means that the entire plan, from the Work Breakdown Structure to the GANTT chart, will have to be adjusted. This redesign is not due to Cory's mismanagement of the project, but because he and the team were not given complete information from the beginning planning steps.

## Rescheduling Dates

Rescheduling means adjusting the calendar dates we have assigned to certain tasks or rescheduling team members' time. Adjusting the calendar dates will happen if task A, which must be completed before task B can start, is not completed on schedule. This will necessitate task B being rescheduled.

# Putting the Plan into Action

**If you want to impact the final completion date of the project, those tasks to which you add or from which you subtract resources must be on the critical path.**

Rescheduling team members' time can happen as a result of illness or other unplanned absences when others must fill in to keep the project on schedule. It can also be done as a result of a decision to throw more staff resources to a specific task in order to get it done faster. The decision to do this can affect other tasks unless the team member(s) are at a point where the tasks they are working on contain some slack. Remember, if you want to impact the final completion date of the project, those tasks to which you add or from which you subtract resources must be on the critical path.

> ## Take a Moment
> Will rescheduling be an option for Cory to consider? Why or why not?
> 
> _____
> 
> _____
> 
> _____

The information we have been given does not specify whether any of the tasks that have fallen behind schedule are on the critical path and, if they do, whether Cory has the option to change the targeted completion date for the total project. If changing the final completion date to a later date would be an option, then he should consider how to move the dates of when these tasks are to be completed, leaving the time to complete each task the same. It may not, however, be possible to change the final completion date, which means that additional team members must be assigned to those critical path tasks that are behind schedule.

## Reallocating Resources

Resources include the space for the project team, equipment, budget, supplies, and team personnel. Reassigning team members to other tasks is reallocating those resources. But it is possible that the other resources may also need to be reallocated.

# Putting the Plan into Action

For example, space for the project team may need to be expanded or reconfigured, or there may be a budget overrun requiring a cut in future planned expenditures. Reallocating resources involves changing the way the resource is to be used. Based on the information given to us, it would appear that team members' time would be the critical issue to deal with at this point. However, it is possible that to bring the project back on schedule, unplanned overtime may be required. This would necessitate reallocating the budget to cover these expenses.

> **Reallocating resources involves changing the way the resource is to be used.**

## Take a Moment

Are there any other resources besides team members' time that Cory should consider reallocating?

_____

_____

_____

_____

## Delegating Tasks

The project manager has many things to keep on top of during the implementation stage. Some of these include:

- Knowing the status of the entire project and individual tasks and communicating this to the team and other interested persons.

- Following up on problem situations as soon as they surface to minimize their impact.

- Keeping ahead of current activities and ensuring that what needs to be done for future activities is being done.

- Monitoring budget expenditures and making adjustments.

- Maintaining good relations with other parts of the company that play an important role in the success of the project (team members' functional bosses, the IT department that supports the equipment the team needs to function, etc.)

• **Putting the Plan into Action**

Sometimes the project manager can feel overwhelmed with the number of things that need to be done and the limited time in which to do them. When this happens, it is time to delegate some of these responsibilities to team members. The project manager must be thoughtful in doing this, however, both in deciding which duties can be delegated and to whom they are delegated.

**Some duties require the personal involvement of the project manager and should not be delegated.**

Some duties require the personal involvement of the project manager and should not be delegated (maintaining good relations with the functional supervisors of the team members). Other duties may require specific skills not held by all team members (identifying problems and knowing what to do to minimize their impact). The project manager must match the task with the appropriate person to carry it out.

### Take a Moment

Would delegating some of Cory's responsibilities have minimized the problems that he is facing? Why or why not?

_____

_____

_____

Cory has not handled the changes that need to be made to the project and has not kept the team and their supervisors in the loop of information on the project status. He could have minimized the problems he is now facing if he had delegated the updating of the GANTT Chart and its distribution. This would have alerted others to the problems and greatly increased the chances of contingent plans being developed sooner.

## Resolving Conflicts

Projects are full of conflicts, and the conflicts are not always between people. Resolving conflicts is a major part of project management, something that many project managers are reluctant to deal with. But ignoring a conflict won't make it go away. It will just become worse and may eventually blow up into a major problem.

# Putting the Plan into Action

Conflict is seldom the result of personality differences between people. It is almost always an issue of the structure in which they are dealing with each other. The structure has created the conflict, not the people. Change the structure, and the conflict often disappears. Here are some typical conflicts the project manager will encounter as he or she manages the project.

> **Conflict is seldom the result of personality differences between people.**

- **Priorities**
  This conflict can occur within the project team or between the team and other groups required to provide support. Establishing clear outcomes and measures during the Inception Stage of the project will go a long way toward minimizing these types of conflict, especially if there is involvement from all parts of the organization that have an investment in the project.

- **Administrative procedures**
  Conflict around these can arise as a result of the project Structure (Partnership, Stand-Alone, Appended) and its inconsistency with the way the rest of the organization does business. Meeting with those parts of the organization that will have the most difficulty dealing with the inconsistency and clarifying how to work together to accomplish project goals will help alleviate potential conflicts.

- **Methodologies and interpretation**
  Disagreements over formulas and methodologies to be used, as well as interpretation of the results of methods and approaches chosen, can cause conflict within the organization as well as the project team. To minimize conflicts, collaboratively select formulas, methodologies, and results interpretation approaches with those parts of the organization that will be affected.

- **Personnel resources**
  People from different departments may disagree about where project staff should come from, the abilities of potential staff members, and the availability of staff time to devote to the project. Critical conflicts over these issues may not ever be resolved without senior management intervention.

### Putting the Plan into Action

- **Budgeting**
  There may be disagreements over the accuracy of cost estimates. All cost data and the processes used to develop them need to be verifiable and open to scrutiny by anyone.

- **Scheduling**
  Problems may arise over the time estimates given on various tasks as well as the sequencing and scheduling of those tasks. Establishing time estimates needs to be a broad-based activity with as much involvement across the organization as possible. Communicating project status and time expectations through the use of GANTT Charts will help minimize conflicts. Give people information.

- **Personality**
  Problems may also arise over differing approaches to doing things and ego issues around control and authority. This is why it is good to have team members with various skills and approaches so that changes in assignments can be made if personality issues arise. Please note that personality accounts for only 10 percent or less of all conflicts. The other conflicts identified above are structural in nature and account for 90 percent of the conflict you'll encounter as a project manager.

> **Take a Moment**
> What kind of conflict is Cory experiencing and how could it be resolved?
>
> _____
>
> _____

The primary conflict that Cory is experiencing at this time is with the team members' functional supervisors over the need for additional staff time. A way to handle this would be to get them all together, lay out the problems with missed deadlines, share Cory's idea as to how the project can be brought back on track, and let the supervisors and team members have input. This will give them some ownership of the revised schedule and minimize future conflicts over team members' time.

## Managing Interfaces

All projects have their own set of outcomes and measures which at some point come in contact with the outcomes and measures of the main organization. That point of contact is considered an interface. In order for the project to be as successful as possible, someone, primarily the project manager, must manage the points of interface to assure that political and organization barriers do not undermine the project.

Interfaces, their needs, and their solutions can be organized around the project stages.

| Stages | Interfacing Needs | Interfacing Solutions |
| --- | --- | --- |
| 1. Inception<br>2. Start-Up | Creating the plan; building teams; establishing objectives; cross-organizational involvement | Macroplanning approach; extensive participation; consensus decision making; kick-off sessions |
| 3. Implementation | Monitor project status; motivation; intensive communication; high visibility | Periodic project review meetings; design reviews; frequent team, sponsor and major players or supporters updates; roll-out planning; training for staff |
| 4. Close | Create close-out plan; transition ongoing tasks; evaluate the project | Involve all needed parties in plan development; create checklist for closing tasks; interview staff, sponsors, and major players/supporters |

● **Putting the Plan into Action**

> **Take a Moment**
> 
> During which stage or stages did Cory fail to appropriately manage the interfaces? According to the chart, what would have been the appropriate solution?
> 
> _____
> 
> _____
> 
> _____

Cory did not manage the interfaces during the Inception and Start-Up Stages. Information vital to the project was not made available to the team for their planning. This could have been prevented if Cory had had broader involvement in the planning project.

## Chapter Summary

The Implementation Stage is where the project manager begins to manage the project. There are several activities that project managers use to accomplish this:

- **Monitoring progress**
  Using GANTT Charts to monitor the completion of tasks and to communicate their status to team members and others in the organization.

- **Redesigning**
  This can be necessary if tasks are added or eliminated or there are cost overruns. It may be necessary to redo the Work Breakdown Structure, network diagram, and placement on the time line. Or the redesign may not be that extensive.

- **Rescheduling**
  Involves adjusting the calendar dates assigned to certain tasks or rescheduling team members' time.

- **Reallocating resources**
  Resources include space for the project team, equipment, budget, supplies, and team personnel. Any of these may need to be reallocated during the project implementation.

## Putting the Plan into Action

- **Delegating**
  It may be necessary for project manager to delegate duties. This should be done in a thoughtful way, both in deciding which duties can be delegated and to whom they can be delegated.

- **Resolving conflicts**
  Projects are full of conflicts between people. However, only 10 percent of all conflicts are due to personality issues. Structural conflicts account for the other 90 percent and can usually be resolved if the structural problems are resolved.

- **Managing interfaces**
  Project managers must be concerned with and manage those points of contact between the outcomes and measures of the project and those of the rest of the organization.

• **Putting the Plan into Action**

### Self Check: Chapter Seven Review

Answers appear on page 130.

1. What is the primary tool used to monitor the project?
   _____

2. What are some reasons that a project might need to be redesigned?
   a. _____
   
   b. _____
   
   c. _____

3. What are the resources of a project that are available to be reallocated?
   a. _____
   
   b. _____
   
   c. _____
   
   d. _____
   
   e. _____

4. Why must the project manager be thoughtful in delegating duties?
   a. _____
   
   b. _____

# Stage Four: Close

Although briefer than any of the other stages, the close is still important because it determines how the results of a project continue to live and grow either within the organization or as a spin-off from the organization. Or, if the project was canceled, how the lessons learned are captured for future use. This stage is also about the people who have worked on the project and how their futures are secured or assisted.

Tasks to be accomplished during this stage include:

1. Resolving project commitments.
2. Transferring continuing activities.
3. Reassigning project personnel.
4. Conducting a project evaluation.

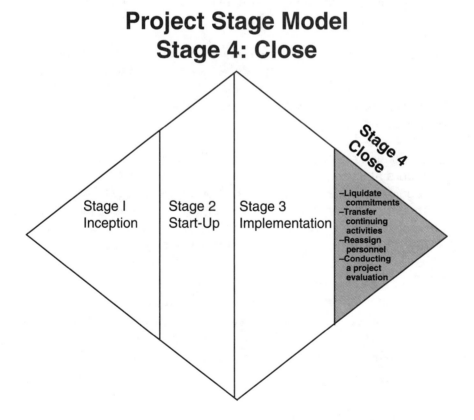

● Concluding the Project

# Chapter *Eight*
## Concluding the Project

### Chapter Objectives

▶ Explain the project manager's responsibilities in closing down a project.

▶ Use the closing project evaluation for future learning.

**Case Study**

Susan is the manager of a project that is starting to wind down. Her team is finishing up the training of company personnel so project results can be transferred to an ongoing operation. Susan herself begins meeting today with areas of the company that have been involved in project implementation so she can evaluate how the process has gone.

One area that is uncertain is what will happen to the office space and equipment that have been used by the project team once the project is over. No one really planned for their distribution after the project, and Susan hopes feelings are not hurt when the final decisions are made.

Susan is also uncertain about what will happen to her team members at the end of the project. She has voiced her concern to her senior manager, but nothing has been decided yet. Team members have begun to ask her whether they will have jobs when the project is over, and she doesn't know what to tell them. "I wish we had thought this all out in advance," she says to herself angrily.

We have now reached the final stage of the project, the Close Stage. Whether it goes smoothly or not depends on the planning that was done during the Inception and Start-Up Stages and how things were carried out during the Implementation Stage. Our opening example shows what can happen when the Close Stage isn't properly planned.

## Concluding the Project

There are four primary tasks to accomplish during the close:

- Liquidate project commitments.
- Transfer continuing activities.
- Reassign project personnel.
- Conduct a project evaluation.

Let's look at each separately and use Susan's project as an example.

## Resolving Project Commitments

Some projects require the purchase or lease of equipment, the lease of space for the project team, and even contracting with some project team members from outside the organization if certain skills or knowledge cannot be found with current employees. Other projects will not have to deal with any of this because all aspects of the project can be accomplished with in-house resources.

For those projects requiring the acquisition of resources through lease, purchase, or contract, this is the phase in which these commitments are terminated. Although not usually difficult, it must be done, and the responsibility, unless delegated, will fall to the project manager. This process will go more smoothly and nothing will fall through the cracks if these tasks are planned for by being included in the project plan when it is developed during the Start-Up Stage. As a project ends and team members and the project manager go on to other duties and responsibilities, these things can drag out or get lost if they have not been included in the project plan.

# Concluding the Project

> **Take a Moment**
> 
> What are the commitments that must be handled by Susan in the scenario at the beginning of the chapter? Does it appear that disposition of these items was included in the project plan?
> 
> _____
> 
> _____
> 
> _____

Although it is not clear if the space and equipment that have been used by the project team were leased or purchased by the company, it does not appear that much thought was given to their disposition during the planning of the project. Unfortunately, they could become a point of contention between various parts of the organization, creating a win-lose outcome in which people are dissatisfied, hurt, offended, or made unhappy because their needs are not considered a priority. This could have been avoided if proper planning had been done and these decision made earlier.

## Transferring Continuing Activities

Projects result in change. The impact of the change on the rest of the organization could be small, or it could be major. But there is always change. Part of the planning process is to recognize this fact and to build into the final stage of the project the means for incorporating this change into the rest of the organization.

How will it blend into existing work units? Have the other units been included all along so that they have ownership of the change and do not feel that it is being imposed upon them? Have the resources necessary to successfully implement the change been planned for so they are available?

## Take a Moment

Have Susan and her team made arrangements to transfer ongoing project activities to other departments? Explain.

_____

_____

_____

As the project is winding down, Susan's team is actively involved in the training and transfer of the project outcomes. It would appear that her team has done an excellent job in planning for this.

## Reassigning Project Personnel

The structure of the project and where the team members came from will determine the specific issues involved in this task.

If the some of the team members are contracted employees hired only for the length of the project, their disposition has been clear to them and the rest of the team from the beginning. They have never had the expectation that they will be needed beyond the end of the project. Reassignment is not an issue in this case.

If the project structure is Appended, there will probably not be any reassignment of in-house employees necessary. This is one of the advantages of this particular structure. If the project structure is Partnership, there also should not be an issue of reassigning personnel. These team members stayed assigned to their functional areas but were released to spend some portion of their time on the project. They have been doing at least some portion of their job during the entire project, so they will just pick up where they left off when they began the project.

The issue of reassigning project personnel becomes a concern if the project has been a Stand-Alone. In some organizations, the disposition of the project team members and project manager is planned for and discussed with the team members before they agreed to be on the team.

# Concluding the Project

But in other organizations, plans are never made and the issue never addressed. As the end of the project draws near, the anxiety level of team members increases. Final tasks can suffer if team members are too anxious to concentrate (or too busy looking for new jobs because they can no longer stand the uncertainty).

Regardless of whether the reassignment of personnel is an issue, the project manager needs to be sensitive to the impact the disbanding of the project team will have on its members. Team members will feel a true sense of loss, greater for a longer and more time-intensive project. There should be some sort of acknowledgment of this through a celebration, statement of appreciation, or some other means of formally acknowledging team members' participation.

## Take a Moment
What project structure was used for Susan's project? If you were the project manager, what would you have done differently to prevent the situation in the scenario from happening?

_____

_____

_____

Because of the anxiety being expressed by the team members, Susan's project has probably been a Stand-Alone. The disposition of the team members after the project has not been planned. It may not always be possible for the project manager to obtain a guarantee from senior management on the disposition of the team during the Inception or Start-Up Stages. But this does not relieve the project manager from the responsibility of pressing for a decision on this throughout the project.

# Concluding the Project

## Evaluating the Project

Sometimes the evaluation of the project is ignored because it is the final thing to be done and will not really impact the success or failure of this project. But it is an important activity because of the information that can be gained for the next project the organization undertakes.

We have included some questions that can be used to evaluate a project. But this is not an exhaustive list, and many more questions that apply to a specific project could be added. These questions should be answered by the project manager, the project team, and any others within the organization who were involved with the project.

## Project Evaluation Questions

1. Was the project completed on time?
   - If so, what do you attribute this to?
   - If not, what should have been done differently?

2. Did the project come in within budget?
   - If so, what do you attribute this to?
   - If not, what should have been done differently?

3. Were the goals of the project met?
   - If not, why?

4. What did your interviews with project team members and sponsors reveal regarding satisfaction with the outcome of the project?

5. How did the project structure help and/or hinder project success?

6. What changes would you make in the team selection processes?

7. What changes would you make in the project management processes?

8. Are you satisfied with the type and frequency of communication with the team and other interested people in the organization?
   - What would you do differently next time?

9. Were major conflicts effectively resolved?
   - What, if anything, should you have done differently?

# Concluding the Project

10. Were your procedures for monitoring the project effective?

11. Did the initial project plan and timelines prove to be reasonably accurate and valuable in managing the project?
    - What would you change in the future?

12. Did the time estimates for each task prove to be reasonably accurate?
    - What could you have done to improve them?

13. What did you learn about yourself as a project manager and/or team member?
    - What are your strengths?
    - What are your needs?
    - What can you do to address them?

### Take a Moment
What are some areas of evaluation that you would want to cover in the questions asked about Susan's project?

_____

_____

_____

All of the questions listed above would be appropriate and provide good information for the project manager of the next project in the company. In addition, there should be some questions addressing the issue of reassigning the team since this has become such an important issue in Susan's project.

# Concluding the Project

## Pulling It All Together

This completes the stages and process used to manage projects. We've covered a lot of information, so let's review the main points.

Any project has four stages: Inception, Start-Up, Implementation, and Close. Each stage builds upon the previous stage and has its own set of tasks to accomplish.

### The Inception Stage

In this stage, several key aspects are defined:

- Management's intent
- The project scope
- Desired outcomes
- The structure
- Measures of success
- Who will be the project manager
- Who will be on the project team

### The Start-Up Stage

Here the project staff creates the project plan and sets the budget. The steps consist of:

1. Identifying the work breakdown structure.
2. Determining task relationships.
3. Creating the network diagram.
4. Establishing time needed.
5. Calculating the expected time.
6. Calculating the time for each path.
7. Identifying the critical path.
8. Calculating the slack.
9. Establishing the timeline.
10. Determining the budget.

# Concluding the Project

## The Implementation Stage

In this stage project tasks are completed and the project manager manages the project. The activities of this stage include:

- Monitoring progress
- Redesigning
- Rescheduling
- Reallocating resources
- Delegating
- Resolving conflicts
- Managing interfaces

## The Close Stage

This is the final stage of the project. During this stage, the activities include:

- Liquidating commitments
- Transferring continuing activities
- Reassigning personnel
- Evaluating the project

As the project manager, pay attention to the emotional aspects of the team as they experience the ending of the project.

Good luck with your project!

# Concluding the Project

## Self Check: Chapter Eight Review

Answers to these questions appear on page 131.

1. What are the four primary activities of the close stage?

   a. _____

   b. _____

   c. _____

   d. _____

2. Which project structure will necessitate the reassignment of personnel?

   _____

3. What is the purpose of the project evaluation?

   _____

# Answers to Selected Exercises

## Chapter One (page 18)

1. Ongoing management implies a long-term investment aimed at meeting a constant need. Usually a set of policies and procedures exists to guide the work of staff performing the function. Project management implies a short-term investment aimed at meeting a time-sensitive, object-specific need that may never reoccur. Most often, no policies or procedures exist to guide the work of the project manager or project team.

2. 
   a. Size
   b. Familiarity
   c. Complexity
   d. Consequences

3. 
   a. A defined goal that must be achieved within a certain period of time.
   b. Sequential and interrelated activities.
   c. A defined start and end point.

4. Project managers:
   a. Enjoy the challenge of doing something new.
   b. Like being a change agent.
   c. Like taking risks.
   d. Quickly develop new approaches and create detailed plans.
   e. Enjoy managing dynamic interfaces between people and systems.

## Chapter Two (page 35)

1. A
2. B
3. D
4. C
5. C
6. A
7. B
8. A
9. D
10. C

# Answers to Selected Exercises

11. A
12. A
13. A
14. C
15. C
16. D
17. C
18. A
19. C

## Chapter Three (page 53)

1. B
2. A
3. C
4. A
5. B
6. B
7. C
8. A
9. B

## Chapter Four (page 61)

1. a. Whether project tasks are accomplished.
   b. How the project is managed.

2. S a. Meeting deadlines
   P b. Implementing outcomes
   S c. Maintaining customer confidence
   S d. Creating change
   P e. Gaining buy-in
   S f. Providing access
   A g. Managing risk
   S h. Providing closure

# Answers to Selected Exercises

## Chapter Five (page 72)

1. B. The Stand-Alone Structure
2. C. The Partnership Structure
3. A. The Appended Structure
4. Choose from:
    - Communication skills
    - Relationship-building skills
    - Ability to work on a team
    - Flexibility
    - Openness to change
    - Comfort with the project structure
    - Technical knowledge

## Chapter Six (page 100)

1. F
2. D
3. B
4. E
5. A
6. C
7. $TE = \dfrac{TO + 4TM + TP}{6}$
8. A GANTT Chart

## Chapter Seven (page 115)

1. The GANTT Chart

2. a. An outcome is added or eliminated.
   b. The project has fallen so far behind schedule that a new approach must be taken to complete it.
   c. Costs have risen and must be brought under control.

3. a. Space for the project team
   b. Equipment
   c. Budget
   d. Supplies
   e. Team personnel

4. a. Some duties require the personal involvement of the project manager.
   b. Other duties require specific skills not held by all team members.

# Answers to Selected Exercises

## Chapter Eight (page 127)

1. a. Resolving project commitments
   b. Transferring continuing activities
   c. Reassigning project personnel
   d. Evaluating the project

2. The Stand-Alone Structure

3. To help make the next project better.

# NOTES

# NOTES

# NOTES

# NOTES

# NOTES